DK

First Nature Encyclopedia

DK PUBLISHING, INC.

LONDON, NEW YORK, MUNICH,
MELBOURNE, and DELHI

Written and edited by Caroline Bingham and Ben Morgan
Senior designer Tory Gordon-Harris
Project art editor Laura Roberts-Jensen
Additional design Karen Hood

Publishing manager Susan Leonard
US editor Christine Heilman
Jacket design Victoria Harvey
Picture researcher Mariana Sonnenberg
Production controller Seyhan Esen
DTP designer Almudena Díaz

Consultant Kim Dennis-Bryan Ph.D. FZS

First American edition, 2006
Published in the United States by
DK Publishing, Inc., 375 Hudson Street,
New York, NY 10014

Copyright © 2006 Dorling Kindersley Limited

06 07 08 09 10   10 9 8 7 6 5 4 3 2 1

DK books are available at special discounts for bulk purchases for sales
promotions, premiums, fund-raising, or educational use. For details,
contact: DK Publishing Special Markets, 375 Hudson Street,
New York, NY 10014 or SpecialSales@dk.com

Library of Congress Cataloging-in-Publication Data

First nature encyclopedia.-- 1st American ed.
    p. cm.

Includes index.

ISBN 0-7566-1415-5 (hardcover)

1. Natural history--Encyclopedias, Juvenile. 2. Nature--
Encyclopedias, Juvenile.

QH48.F53 2006
508.03--dc22

2005031875

Color reproduction by Colourscan, Singapore
Printed and bound in China by Toppan

Discover more at
www.dk.com

Contents

Introduction

Polar Regions

Cool Forests

Rainforests

Grasslands

This book will ask you questions at the bottom of each page...

About this book

The pages of this book have special features that will show you how to get your hands on as much information as possible! Look for these:

The Curiosity quiz will get you searching through each section for the answers.

Become-an-expert buttons tell you where to look for more information on a subject.

Every page is color-coded to show you which section it is in.

Get messy
Activities show you how you can try things out for yourself.

Sunflower

Honeybee

The Living World

Nature surrounds us in the form of the living world, a world made up of living things. It is an amazing world.

Life on Earth began

Plants

From the tiniest flower to the largest tree, there are an immense variety of plants. Scientists believe there are about 400,000 species, but it may be many more.

Giant redwood

Flowers

Many plants produce flowers. These are pollinated by animals, wind, and by the plant itself. Pollination results in the seeds needed to grow new plants.

Orchid

Daisy

Plants are able to make their own food.

Plants produce the oxygen we breathe.

Fungi

They may look like plants, but fungi are neither animals nor plants, though they are living things.

Mushrooms and toadstools are fungi.

Which group of animals has the most members?

Owl

Animals

The animal kingdom consists of vertebrates (animals with a backbone) and invertebrates (the creepy-crawlies).

about 2.5 billion years ago.

Green woodpecker

Butterfly

Vulture

Animals with backbones

Vertebrates, or animals with backbones, are divided into five categories.

 Mammals breathe air. Most live on land, but some are aquatic.

Birds have feathered wings. Most can fly, but some can't (like the penguin).

Reptiles are cold-blooded and rely on their environment for body heat.

Amphibians are able to live on land or in water. They are cold-blooded.

 Fish live in fresh water or sea water—or some can move between the two.

Elephant

Moth

Penguin

Orangutan

Unlike plants, animals have to find their own food.

Kangaroo

Swan

Red fox

Badger

Starfish

Toad

Snail

Tortoise

5

The invertebrates: they make up 97 percent of all animal species.

World Habitats

Animals and plants survive in an immense variety of habitats, from the frozen Arctic to tropical rainforests near the equator.

Polar bear

Deciduous leaf

Butterfly

Zebra

Polar Regions

The areas immediately around the North and South poles are frozen deserts, but move a little farther out and plenty of animals live with the ice.

Cool Forests

Parts of the world have seasons: spring, summer, fall, and winter. It is an environment in which broad-leaved, or deciduous, trees flourish.

Rainforests

In areas of land near the equator, it is hot and humid. This is where you will find the tropical rainforests, full of colorful plants and animals.

Grasslands

There are about 10,800 species of grass. Huge areas of grassland attract grass-eating animals, which attract predators such as lions and cheetahs.

What is a habitat?

Deserts

Sidewinder

One-seventh of all land is desert. At first sight, a desert may seem barren, but desert plants and animals have some surprising ways of surviving.

Mountains and Caves

Golden eagle

Mountains cover five percent of all land. Plants and animals living on a mountain have to cope with less oxygen, severe cold, and strong winds.

Fresh Water

Lily

The world is full of freshwater lakes, rivers, and streams, all fed by rainwater. These habitats attract all sorts of insects, animals, and plants.

Oceans

Fish

Earth is largely made up of oceans. Animals and some plants flourish in this salty world. Most sea life is found in shallow water and around coral reefs.

Towns and Cities

Pigeon

From mosses growing in brick walls to rats rooting through our garbage, many plants and animals have settled in our towns and cities.

A habitat is the place or environment where particular organisms live.

The Poles

Earth's polar regions are harsh habitats. The land animals here are warm-blooded, which means they keep their body at a constant temperature that is higher than that of their surroundings.

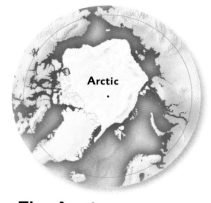

Arctic

Antarctic

Cold-blooded animals such as snakes and frogs would not survive at the poles. They'd freeze solid.

The Arctic
The Arctic lies around the North Pole, with most of the region taken up by the Arctic Ocean. Large sheets of ice cover much of the Arctic Ocean.

The Antarctic
The South Pole is in the middle of a continent: Antarctica. Ninety-eight percent of Antarctica is covered by ice.

Polar bears live in the Arctic. They are good swimmers.

Polar bear

How often does the sun rise each year at the North Pole?

Ice does float!

Icebergs are huge pieces of floating ice, but what you see is really just the tip of an iceberg. This makes them very dangerous to ships.

Polar ice is formed from fresh water.

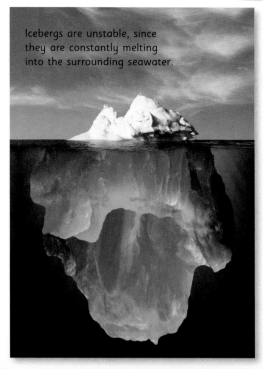

Icebergs are unstable, since they are constantly melting into the surrounding seawater.

Land of the midnight sun

Polar regions stay light for 24 hours a day in summer, but they remain cloaked in darkness in the winter. This is because of Earth's orbit around the Sun.

Antarctica has 70 percent of the world's fresh water, but is as dry as a desert.

Curiosity quiz

Look through the Polar Regions pages and see if you can identify the picture clues below.

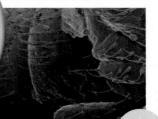

Become an expert...

on Antarctica, pages **14-15**
on icy seas, pages **110-111**

Once—because of Earth's position in relation to the Sun.

Life in the Freezer

Polar regions are often dark, blasted by freezing winds, and they receive little rain. Only the toughest can survive.

Polar bears have thick blubber under their skin to help keep the cold out.

Polar bear

Although their fur is white, polar bears have black skin.

Let's stay warm
Penguins huddle together to stay warm. The adults and chicks on the outside of the huddle aren't so well protected from the cold, so they take turns standing in the middle.

Polar giants
Large animals lose heat more slowly than small ones, so many Arctic animals are big. A male polar bear can be 8 ft (2.5 m) long and weigh 0.9 tons (800 kg).

To survive blizzards, muskoxen simply sit down and wait, using as little energy as possible.

Muskoxen may look like cattle, but they are actually goats!

A walking coat
The muskox looks like a small, shaggy-haired buffalo. Its coat, said to be eight times warmer than sheep's wool, is made of coarse hairs as long as your arm.

What is the world's largest bear?

One big cover-up

Many polar animals have thick coats. The snowy owl has feathers on its body that grow long enough to cover its legs and its bill.

Snowy owl

A fine fur coat

The Arctic fox's luxurious fur even covers the soles of its feet. This fox is dark in the summer and white in the winter. In the summer it is very busy, collecting and storing food for the winter.

Cushion growth

It's not just animals that need to wrap up warm—plants do too. Purple saxifrage has lots of tiny, overlapping leaves that completely cover the short stems.

Purple saxifrage is one of the first Arctic plants to flower when the snow melts in June.

The snowy owl's talons are perfectly shaped for gripping a lemming.

Polar regions are dark for half the year, but many animals survive.

Become an expert...

on other ways animals survive snow and ice, pages 26-27

It's best to stay under!

Lemmings cope with the cold by staying in tunnels below the snow, where they hunt for plant roots to nibble. If they emerge, they may be caught by a passing snowy owl.

The polar bear.

Arctic Tundra

Arctic tundra bursts into life in the summer, when the surface of the frozen ground melts into a patchwork of boggy pools and meadows.

The sea eagle

In summer, the tundra's pools and rich coasts are a magnet for birds. Steller's sea eagle is one of the top predators.

The sea eagle is a powerful bird and can swoop down to pluck particularly large fish from the water.

Low profile

Arctic plants grow low to the ground.

Lichen is a crusty-looking combination of a fungus and a plant.

Bearberries provide a valuable food for bears in late summer.

Dryas' yellow flowers are shaped like satellite dishes. They track the Sun.

Reindeer moss is a fluffy kind of lichen that grows among other plants.

Cotton grass is one of the most common Arctic plants.

The hare's winter coat is white. A spring molt produces a gray-black coat.

Arctic hare

Insect attack

Hordes of biting insects plague the tundra. Black flies and mosquitoes will cloud around reindeer and suck their blood, while botflies infest their throats.

Hare today

The Arctic hare spends much of its time foraging for food—so much time that a mother visits her litter to suckle them for just two minutes every 18 hours.

Are there any trees in the Arctic?

Some reindeer populations migrate almost 750 miles (1,200 km) twice a year.

Reindeer

These large deer survive by eating grasses and tree saplings in the summer, and scraping back the snow to graze on mosses and lichens in the winter.

Reindeer are the only deer in which both males and females have antlers.

Reindeer

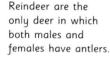

Reindeer are also known as caribou.

The subsoil is permanently frozen, so only shallow-rooted plants can grow.

Follow the herd

Some reindeer herds follow long migration routes into the tundra in summer to feed on the newly sprouted plants and to calve. In winter, they move south.

A large male may stand 5 ft (1.5 m) at the shoulders.

Reindeer hairs are hollow, which helps to trap heat and keep the reindeer warm.

No. Trees can't grow because their roots can't penetrate the frozen ground.

Around Antarctica

Antarctica is Earth's coldest and driest continent. There is little plant life, so nearly all the animals depend on the sea for food.

On the move
Antarctica's ice flows very slowly from the center outward. It takes about 50,000 years for a snowflake at the South Pole to reach the ocean.

Penguin paradise
Only Adélie, gentoo, chinstrap, and emperor penguins nest on the Antarctic continent, but many more species nest on nearby islands.

Emperor penguin

Walking home
Emperor penguins raise their families up to 50 miles (80 km) inland in Antarctica. This means they face a very long walk to reach the sea for fishing trips.

A patient father
The male emperor penguin cares for the egg and then the chick. The chick stays on its father's feet for several months. If it falls, it can freeze to death in just two minutes.

How big is the albatross?

Seals of the south

Six types of seals are found on and around Antarctica. They have few natural enemies, so the colonies thrive.

Crabeater seal

Let's go sieving

Crabeater seals actually eat krill, not crabs, using their teeth to strain these small, shrimplike creatures out of the water.

Southern elephant seal

That's some seal!

The world's largest seal is the male southern elephant seal, which grows to 18 feet (6 m) long. It can reach the weight of two average-sized cars.

A permanent resident

Springtails are insectlike creatures that have spring-loaded tails to catapult them through the air. They are one of the very few Antarctic land-based animals.

Magnified picture of an Antarctic springtail

Antarctic hairgrass

Antarctic hairgrass is one of only two flowering plant species to survive in Antarctica.

Penguins look ungainly when on land.

Just wandering

The wandering albatross has the largest wingspan of any bird. Some pairs nest on islands around Antarctica, usually producing a chick every two years.

Emperor penguins

On route to the sea, penguins will often waddle in single file. They sometimes fall on their bellies and push themselves along.

Its wingspan is 12 feet (2.5 m).

Cool Forests

A forest is a thickly wooded area. Forests have a wide variety of plants and animals living among the trees.

Cool forests are found near the equator at high altitudes, as well as in colder regions.

Weasel

Northern Hemisphere

Coniferous forests

Deciduous forests

Equator

Southern Hemisphere

Where in the world?

Forests that like cooler climates are found largely in the Northern Hemisphere, far north of the equator.

Forest animals
Forests are havens for wildlife, including the weasel, which is small enough to chase small rodents such as mice and voles down their holes.

What name is given to forests that are found near the equator?

What kind of tree?

Forests in cooler climates are made up of two basic types of trees.

Deciduous trees have broad, flat leaves. They lose their leaves in winter.

Coniferous trees don't lose their leaves in winter. They are called evergreens.

Foxglove

Forest plants

Forest floors are shady places, and it can be hard for plants to grow. Plants such as foxgloves can sometimes be found in clearings.

Forests are full of dead wood, which attracts all sorts of creatures.

Curiosity quiz

Look through the Cool Forests pages and see if you can identify the picture clues below.

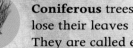

Become an expert...

on deciduous trees, pages **18-19**
on coniferous trees, pages **22-23**

Tropical rainforests.

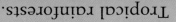

Deciduous Forests

Deciduous trees lose their leaves in winter. These trees need weather patterns that are neither too hot nor too cold, and with seasons.

Layer on layer

Deciduous forests have two or three layers: a canopy (treetops), sometimes a layer of shrubs, and then the low-lying plants such as mosses, ferns, and spring flowers.

If conditions are right, mosses will grow on the north side of a forest tree.

Springing to life

A forest appears to sleep in winter, but in spring it bursts into life. Buds open and ferns spread out to soak up the light.

Land of plenty

A forest floor is littered with dead leaves and wood, and there are often plenty of nuts and berries—it's a perfect hunting ground for squirrels.

The gray squirrel will collect and store acorns and other seeds.

Why do squirrels have bushy tails?

Links in a chain

Food chains connect a species with what it eats.

Leaves act like solar panels to gather sunlight to make food.

Caterpillars—and many other insects—chew on leaves. That's their food.

Birds hunt caterpillars, especially in spring when they have chicks to feed.

Foxes prey on birds, small mammals, and other creatures.

Maple leaf

A leaf is a tree's food factory. In fall, it begins to shut down.

Fall colors

In the growing season, deciduous leaves appear green because of a chemical called chlorophyll. In fall, the leaves turn yellow, brown, or red as the chlorophyll is destroyed.

Woodpeckers have thick skulls to protect against the shock as they hammer into wood.

Woodpecker

Making an entrance

Woodpeckers use their beaks to dig out grubs and to make nest holes. They have amazingly long tongues to probe and seek out insects.

When mature, a fern bud unrolls and the leaflets open out.

Trees as homes

Woodpeckers take two to three weeks to dig out a nest hole, into which the female lays several eggs. The hole is usually in a dead tree.

A squirrel's tail helps it to balance as it leaps from tree to tree.

The Forest Floor

A deciduous forest floor is alive with a mighty army of insects and small creatures. There are rich pickings to be had for these animals.

Catkins

Fern

Male stag beetles have huge mandibles that form "antlers."

Mice nibble on seeds and berries.

Mosses thrive on damp, shady rocks and tree trunks.

Prickly hogs

Hedgehogs snuffle along using their sharp sense of smell to find such goodies as beetles, caterpillars, earthworms, snails, slugs, and spiders.

Earthworm

Things that wriggle

Earthworms help to break soil down, taking it in at their mouth and digesting it in a short intestine. The worms' droppings help to enrich the soil.

European hedgehogs are most active at night, especially when the ground is wet and worms come to the surface.

Seeds

Trees have a variety of ways of spreading their seeds widely.

Rowan trees produce seeds in berries that are eaten and spread by birds.

Poplar seeds grow on catkins. Hairs catch the breeze and they fly away.

Maple seeds have wings that direct their fall away from the tree.

Acorns are collected and buried by squirrels. Some will grow.

How large do stag beetles grow?

Shade lovers

Most plants need lots of sunlight to grow well, but some flourish in shade. These include ferns.

Salamanders breathe through their moist skin, so they have to stay damp all the time.

I'll have your food!

Some plants manage without light by stealing food instead of using sunlight to make food. Broom rape plants grow suckers that work into the roots of other plants.

Broom rape

Woodlice eat rotting plants, fungi—and their own poop!

A stag beetle lays its eggs on decaying tree stumps or roots. The larvae then eat the wood.

A millipede has a tough exoskeleton. Some protect themselves by rolling into a ball.

Stag beetle larva

Life as a larva

A stag beetle spends the first few years of its life as a larva. As an adult, it only survives for a few months.

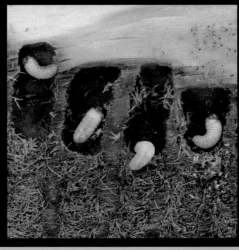

Life in a log

Rotting wood provides food for thousands of tiny animals. Beetle grubs tunnel through it, eating as they go. The grubs are an important food for songbirds.

21

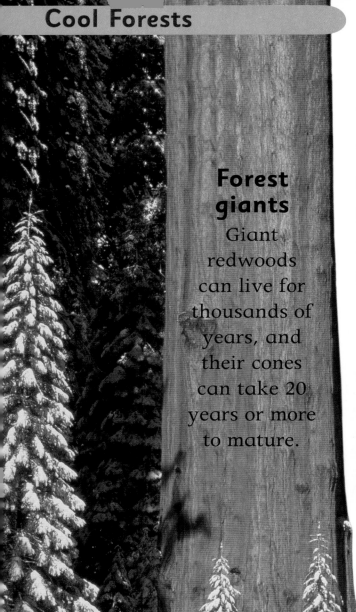

Coniferous Forests

Coniferous forests cover about a tenth of the world's land. In the far north, they form a vast ring around the tundra and North Pole.

Forest giants
Giant redwoods can live for thousands of years, and their cones can take 20 years or more to mature.

Perfectly at home
The North American porcupine is one of the few animals that can eat pine needles. It is also good at climbing the trees.

Cone specialist
Most birds wait for pine cones to fall before eating the seeds, but the crossbill can pry open a conifer's cones with its cross-tipped beak.

Conifer trees are often cone-shaped. This lets snow slide easily off the branches.

Crossbill

What is the world's biggest deer?

Pins and needles

Conifers have needle-shaped leaves that stay on all year. Instead of growing flowers and fruits, they produce cones.

A cone's scales close in wet weather but open when it's dry, releasing the seeds.

Wolverines are also known as gluttons because of their large appetites.

Wolverine

Gray wolf

Wolves and wolverines

Larger predators such as wolves and wolverines are not often spotted in the wild. Thick fur allows them to survive the chilly winters of a coniferous forest.

Does it have antlers?

One of the largest coniferous forest residents is the moose. Only the males have antlers.

Water babies

In summertime, moose love to wade into lakes and ponds to feed on aquatic plants and to escape the clouds of biting flies that suck their blood.

All moose have a "bell" (a flap of skin) hanging from their throat.

The moose (called the elk in Europe).

Fantastic Forest Fungi

Many people think mushrooms are plants, but they are neither plants nor animals. They are, however, living things that need food to stay alive. They love damp forests.

What is a mushroom?

Many fungi live underground. To produce more fungi, they push up mushrooms that send spores into the air.

This mushroom is the visible part of a large fungus that lives underground.

Cep mushroom

Fairy rings

Some fungi are huge and lie like carpets underneath the forest floor. In clearings, mushrooms will sometimes grow around the edge of the unseen fungi in rings.

Puffball

Birds-nest fungi

Bracket fungi

Coral fungi

Cup fungi

Is that a mushroom?

Not all mushrooms look like the mushrooms that you eat. There are many different types, and they come in all shapes, sizes, and colors.

Truffle

Making more fungi

Mushrooms and the other fungi "fruits" do not make seeds. Instead, they make tiny spores that blow away in the wind and produce more fungi.

How big is the biggest fungus in the world?

The fungus family

There are many types of fungi: some you may like, and others you may not.

Penicillin: antibiotics made from fungi can cure diseases in humans.

Mold: when food rots, it sometimes gets mold on it. This is a fungus.

Blue cheese: when you eat blue cheese, you are actually eating mold!

Ringworm: some fungi cause diseases, such as this ringworm on the skin.

Cleaning up

Fungi are one of the world's natural cleaners. When a plant or animal dies, fungi help to break it down, helping to clear the forest of rotten things.

Warning! Poison!

Some mushrooms are very poisonous. They are often brightly colored to warn animals not to eat them. People often call poisonous mushrooms toadstools.

Some poisonous mushrooms can kill a human if eaten.

Fly agaric mushroom

Live food

Some fungi live off the things that they live on, such as trees. They do not have stomachs; instead, they release a liquid that digests food outside the body.

Shaggy ink cap

If mushrooms and toadstools didn't exist, Earth would be buried in several feet (metres) of rotten gunk and life on the planet would soon disappear.

Get messy
Take a large mushroom and cut off the stalk. Lay it on a piece of light paper, cover with a bowl, and leave it for a few days. When you lift the bowl, you will have a spore print.

The world's largest fungus covers an area the size of more than 1,800 football fields.

Winter Survival

The chill of winter brings less food and icy winds. Plants and animals have different techniques for surviving the changes.

Holly

Ivy

Leaves to last

Holly and ivy can survive wintry conditions because their leaves have a thick waxy covering that protects them in both cold and dry weather.

Robin

To stay or go?

Some birds are at home in cold conditions. Male European robins winter in England, while some females fly to milder Spain. Come spring, they will head back.

Let's change color

A number of animals change their coat in the winter. The stoat's coat turns white, for camouflage. A white stoat is known as an ermine.

The stoat has a brown and white summer coat, with a black tip to its tail.

Become an expert...

on survival in extreme cold, pages 10-11

In hibernation, a European dormouse's heart beats just once a minute.

Stoat

A European dormouse spends just five months of the year out of hibernation.

Chilling out

A good way to survive winter is to "hibernate." A hibernating animal isn't just asleep— its body becomes cold and inactive, as though the animal were dead.

Can you name some animals that hibernate?

The great escape

Birds can't hibernate, but they can fly away and spend winter somewhere warmer. Many do this.

Some butterflies hibernate while others spend the winter in chrysalis form, emerging in the spring.

Swallowtail butterfly

Coniferous trees can survive areas where the winters may last eight months.

A hot bath

One group of Japanese macaques jumps into natural hot springs to warm up in winter, though getting out can leave them a bit cold.

Macaques are also known as snow monkeys. The young learn to roll snowballs—just for fun!

Life as a Japanese macaque

In the winter months, Japanese macaques grow a thicker coat. They are intelligent and sociable animals, living in troops of 20 to 30 individuals.

Woodchucks and some bats hibernate.

Weird Woods

Not all evergreen trees have needle-shaped leaves, and not all broad-leaved trees shed their leaves.

Weird woods have some unusual residents, such as the Tasmanian sugar glider.

Tasmanian sugar glider

Panda

Bamboo is broad-leaved, but evergreen.

Bamboo forests

In parts of China, bamboos grow as tall as trees, although they are grasses. They are the fastest-growing plants in the world.

Pandas depend on bamboo forests for their survival.

No need for flight

Many of New Zealand's birds, like the kiwi, are flightless. The kiwi lives more like a hedgehog, rooting around on the forest floor.

Kiwi

Why is the kiwi flightless?

Koala

Life in a tree

Eucalyptus leaves are poisonous, but one animal can stomach them: the koala. Special bacteria aid digestion.

Eucalyptus is broad-leaved, but evergreen.

Tree ferns were once a source of food for some dinosaurs.

Seen by dinosaurs

With their rounded tops and stiff, upward-pointing leaves, monkey-puzzle trees are related to trees that were viewed by dinosaurs. They are broad-leaved, but evergreen.

Prehistoric!

The tree fern is a strange relic from the days of the dinosaurs. It is an evergreen tree.

Ancient monkey-puzzle trees in Chile

Because it has no natural predators.

Rainforests

Tropical rainforests are rich habitats for a huge variety of plants and animals. Enter a hot, damp, and shady world.

Parakeet

Time for the umbrella
A rainforest is warm and sticky, with frequent downpours. The trees take up much of the rain, but water vapor soon evaporates from their leaves, filling the air with moisture.

Queen Alexandra birdwing butterfly (female)

Orangutan

Bursting with life
Tropical rainforests cover just 7% of Earth's land, yet contain over half of the world's species.

Beetles One scientist found 18,000 species of beetles in one small area of rainforest.

Trees A football-field-sized patch of rainforest may contain 300 trees.

Orchids New orchids are continually being discovered in rainforests.

Birds The Amazon alone contains a third of Earth's 9,000 known bird species.

Slipper orchid

Where do most of a rainforest's animals live?

Rainforest layers

A rainforest is like an apartment building, with different residents in different layers. There are four main levels.

Emergents are the high treetops that poke out above everything else.

The canopy is made up from the majority of the treetops. It is a forest's leaky roof.

The understory is made up of short trees, shade-loving plants, and lianas.

The forest floor is a thick carpet of dead leaves, ferns, and the buttresses of tree roots.

Cloud forest

In mountainous areas, rainforests may be so high that they're cloaked in clouds. The heavy moisture encourages lush plant growth.

Eastern rosella

Moth orchid

Curiosity quiz

Look through the Rainforests pages and see if you can identify the picture clues below.

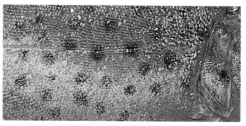

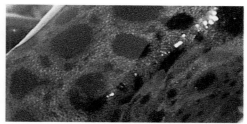

Become an expert...

on other types of forests, pages 16-17

Most of a rainforest's animals (excluding worms in the leaf litter) live in the canopy.

In the Treetops

Climbing plants called lianas snake their way through the canopy.

Much of the life in a rainforest exists way up in the canopy. It is a refreshingly breezy but sunny place to live.

Passion flower

Survival at the top

Many rainforest plants have to compete for light. Some do so by starting life on top of other plants.

Bird's nest anthurium

Crystal anthurium

This tree bra is covered w epiphytes, air pla

A weighty problem

Plants that grow on tree trunks are called epiphytes. Epiphytes can eventually grow so heavy that a branch may fall under their weight.

Bromeliads provide a home for lots of small creatures.

A green bucket

Bromeliads are a type of epiphyte. Their leaves form a tight circle that catches rainwater. Their roots are purely for holding on—they do not steal the host tree's nutrients.

Are there many flowers in the canopy?

Siamangs are the largest of all gibbons. Many gibbons live in the trees.

Siamang

Getting around

Animals have solved the problem of getting from treetop to treetop in a variety of ingenious ways.

Gibbons swing from tree to tree using their hands to grip and hold.

Monkeys scamper around. Some use their tails as an extra limb.

Lemurs make bold leaps between trees, using their long tails for balance.

Birds fly from branch to branch, ready to take off if danger threatens.

Kuhl's flying gecko glides through the air, using its webbed feet.

Flying snakes have flattish bodies and form an S-shape to let them glide.

Tree kangaroos use long claws on their hands to grip tree branches.

Orangutans swing on lianas, or use their weight to bend small trees down.

Aracaris will eat more than 100 different types of fruit, if they can find them.

Nutcrackers

The canopy is full of fruits and nuts all year. Many animals and birds specialize in getting at this food.

Chestnut-eared aracari

Pocket-sized monkey

The pygmy marmoset is the world's smallest monkey. It lives in the treetops of the Amazon jungle, searching for fruits and insects.

It's good for us

Many rainforest seeds are poisonous. Macaws get around this by eating clay before their seed meal. A mineral in the clay absorbs the poisons in the seeds.

Clay

Yes. Some canopy plants flower six times a year.

In the Shade

The understory and forest floor are darker and damper than the canopy. With still air and little or no direct sunlight, they provide a haven for moisture-loving plants and animals.

Coconut crab

Crabs in trees

On some rainforest-covered islands, crabs climb trees and scurry over the forest floor, looking for dead bodies to scavenge.

See-through butterflies

Glasswings are delicate butterflies that live in gloomy parts of the understory.

Glasswing butterfly

Rafflesia

What a stink

Sumatra's rafflesia is the world's biggest flower, though it is more like a fungus. Its rotten smell attracts the insects that pollinate it. The flower lasts for just one week.

How big can a rafflesia grow?

Death by suffocation

Boa constrictors don't have fangs or poison, so they kill prey by squeezing until the animal dies of suffocation.

Boa constrictor eating a rat

A chameleon's eyes can swivel in different directions.

Shy and secretive

Troops of silverback mountain gorillas roam African rainforests during the day. These secretive forest animals spend most of their time on the forest floor.

Jackson's chameleon

Stick to me

Chameleons have extremely long tongues. A thick, sticky pad on the end means a quick end for the chameleon's victim.

Forest flavors

Many of the flavorings we use in food come from rainforest understory plants.

Chocolate comes from the beans of the South American cacao tree.

Vanilla ice cream gets its flavor from the seed pods of a climbing orchid.

Ginger snaps are flavored with the root of a plant from S E Asia.

Killer plant

The strangler fig starts life in a large tree as an epiphyte. Over the years, it wraps roots around the host's trunk and gradually chokes the tree to death.

After the host's death, the strangler's roots will remain as a hollow cage.

Strangler fig enveloping a tree trunk

Rafflesia flowers grow to about 3 ft (1 m) in width.

Red-eyed
tree frog

Red-eyed
tree frog

Crazy Frogs

Warm, damp rainforests make an ideal home for frogs and toads, and there is an almost endless variety of these creatures.

Frogs have four fingers on each of their front limbs, and five on their hind limbs.

Red-eyed tree frog

Leaping for safety

Tree frogs have much longer back legs than front, so they can leap away from danger—or leap in pursuit of a tasty fly.

Sticky fingers

Tree frogs have swollen fingertips with sticky suction cups so they can cling to leaves and twigs.

I can fly!

Wallace's flying frog has huge webbed feet that act like tiny parachutes when it jumps through the air, allowing it to glide. It can "fly" a whopping 50 ft (15 m)!

Hiding from danger

Many rainforest animals enjoy eating frogs and toads, so they need to protect themselves. One way is to use camouflage.

The Asian horned toad almost disappears on a bed of rotting leaves.

What's the difference between a frog and a toad?

Goliath frog

Reaching the size of a cat, the world's largest frog is the goliath. This monster lives in the rainforests of west Africa.

Emerald glass frog

Baby matters

Some rainforest frogs have unusual ways of helping their young to survive. These amphibians don't simply hatch as tadpoles in ponds.

Gastric brooding frogs swallow their tadpoles, releasing them when grown.

Rain frogs develop inside their eggs, stuck to the leaf of a tree.

Surinam toad females carry their eggs on their back, beneath their skin.

Translucent skin

Glass frogs are almost see-through, which helps them to blend in with their surroundings. These curious-looking frogs live in trees that overhang water.

Green poison-dart frog

Yellow-banded poison-dart frog

Blue poison-dart frog

Poison-dart frogs

Some of the most colorful of all frogs use their patterning as a warning that they are extremely poisonous to eat.

Poison-dart frogs eat poisonous insects and store the poison in their skin.

Poison-dart frog

Become an expert...

on tadpole development in a freshwater pond, page **90**

There's no clear difference. Toads typically have warty skin.

Praying mantis

Praying for dinner
The praying mantis hunts by stealth. It remains motionless, then springs forward to catch its victim.

The victim, a fly, is caught before it has a chance to react.

Jungle Bugs

Rainforests are home to more species of insects than anywhere else. They include the biggest, deadliest, loudest, and weirdest!

Leafcutter ants form pathways

Farming the forest
Leafcutter ants cannot eat the leaves they carry back home. They harvest them to grow a fungus, which they eat.

Leafcutter ants

Let me eat, eat, eat
Butterflies are a common sight in rainforests. This means there are lots of caterpillars to spot—chubby little eating machines.

Giraffe beetle

Stick your neck out
The giraffe weevil has an extraordinarily long neck, but nobody knows why! It can bend its neck to look under leaves.

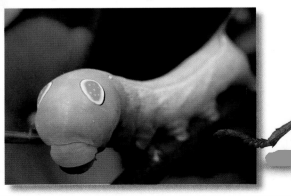

How many insect species exist?

Living jewels

Iridescent markings help this
butterfly find a mate in the forest.
The flash of bright color may also
confuse a bird that wants to eat it.

This morpho has a
wingspan of about
4 in (10 cm).

**Blue
morpho**

to carry leaves to their nest.

Record-breakers

When it comes to bugs,
rainforests are home
to many of the world's
record-breakers.

African goliath beetles
are the heaviest insects,
reaching 3$\frac{1}{2}$ oz (100 g).

**Brazil's goliath bird-
eating spider** is the
world's largest spider.

**Malaysia's giant stick
insect** can reach 22 in
(55.5 cm) in length.

This **click beetle** produces
the most light of any
insect—enough to read by!

Mosquitoes are the
deadliest insects, spreading
a sickness called malaria.

**Queen Alexandra's
birdwing butterfly** is
huge, reaching 11 in (28 cm).

Tasty tears

Butterflies visit flowers
to feed on nectar, but
nectar is short of salt
and other minerals.
These butterflies
are collecting those
missing minerals
from a turtle's eyes
and nostrils.

Spikes on this
nymph's head,
body, and legs
help it to look like
a thorny plant.

Alien empire

Some insects hide from
danger by disguising
themselves as leaves
and sticks.

**Stick insect
nymph**

More than a million species have been identified.

Night Life

If you venture into a rainforest at night, you will soon realize that the forest never sleeps...

Macuna flowers

Underwood's long-tongued bat

Vampire bat

Night flowers

Some flowers, like the shaving-brush tree, are pollinated by bats, so they only open at night.

Shaving-brush tree

If a flower looks like a brush, it's probably pollinated by bats!

Vampire bat

A vampire bat's saliva contains anesthetic, so the victim doesn't feel the bat lapping up their blood.

Atlas moth

The atlas moth is the world's largest moth.

Mega moths

The nighttime rainforest is full of moths, which flit around trying to find flowers or each other—using their incredible sense of smell.

Uraniid moth

Butler's brahmin

A ghostly nighttime glow will attract insects.

Fairy lanterns?

These strange, glowing lights on the forest floor are luminous mushrooms.

Why do moths fly into lights?

Seeing in the dark

Bushbabies have huge eyes to help them see at night. Their eyes are sensitive, so they avoid bright light, which can damage their eyes.

Golden eyelash viper

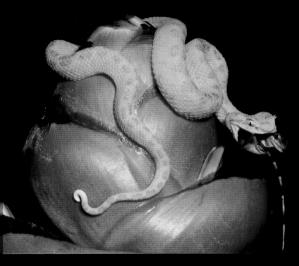

Bushbaby

Slippery snake

Snakes can hunt in complete darkness, using their tongue to taste the air for the smell of prey. The eyelash viper also has special heat-sensing pits on its head.

Ocelot

On the prowl

Many rainforest animals are nocturnal, which means they wake up at night and begin to hunt.

An ocelot hunts with its head lowered to pick up the scent of its prey.

Get messy

Make a moth trap. Lean empty egg cartons inside a box. Light the box with a flashlight and leave outdoors at night. In the morning, you may find moths hiding under the egg cartons.

They mistake them for stars and think they're flying upward.

Rainforest Rivers

Rainforest rivers are frequently muddied by the amount of silt that washes into them following rain, but many animals make a good life in them.

Through the jungle
Rivers snake through rainforests, carrying excess rainwater toward the ocean.

Amazon river dolphin

Rubber neck

The Amazon river dolphin has a very flexible neck. It uses this ability to get around tree roots.

Red-bellied piranhas

Dangerous fish

A shoal of red-bellied piranhas can strip an animal to the bone in seconds. They eat by slicing off chunks of flesh, using their sharp, triangular teeth.

Nine-banded armadillo

Are all piranhas dangerous?

Just another catfish

There is a huge variety of catfish—in fact, three-fourths of all freshwater fish are catfish or related to catfish. This catfish reaches about 2 ft (60 cm) in length.

Shovel-nosed tiger catfish

Walking on water
The basilisk lizard can run on water. As basilisks get older, they get too heavy and can't run so far on water.

Anacondas squeeze their prey to death.

A giant in the river

The world's heaviest snake is the green anaconda. A snake this size is capable of killing deer and caimans.

Green anaconda

Walking underwater
The nine-banded armadillo is able to walk under water. It can hold its breath while it crosses a narrow stream. Its armor provides a tough defense.

This armadillo has nine bands of bony carapace between its shoulder and rump.

What a whopper

The giant otter can grow to almost 6 ft (2 m) in length, making it the world's largest otter. River otters use rocks as hammers to smash shells.

No. Most piranha species are harmless.

Jungles of Asia

Southeast Asia's rainforests are spread over a number of islands and contain some animals found nowhere else.

Monkey cup pitcher plant

A rare sight

The Sumatran rhino is one of the rarest animals of all—just 300 or so exist. It is also the smallest and hairiest of all rhinos, although its coat of hair is rather sparse.

Ready for lunch

Pitcher plants contain small pools of syrupy liquid. Insects fall into the pools and drown.

A suit of armor

The pangolin hides in a burrow by day and emerges to hunt at night. Its scales form a flexible shield.

Malaysian pangolin

Person of the forest

Orangutans are closely related to human beings and chimpanzees, and they are just as clever as chimps. They spend much of their life in trees, even making a nest and sleeping there.

Clouded leopard

The clouded leopard is one of the only cats that can climb down a tree headfirst—it rarely gets stuck!

Does a pangolin have teeth?

The Rajah Brook's wings are shaped rather like a bird's wings.

Rajah Brook's birdwing butterfly

Clinging to a tree trunk, a tarsier hunts for prey.

Jewel of the forest

This spectacular butterfly has a wingspan about the length of your hand. When large groups of birdwings gather to drink from puddles, it's a very pretty sight.

Ever watchful

Instead of moving its eyes like us, a tarsier can turn its head 180° in both directions to look behind it.

The clouded leopard's prey includes monkeys, gibbons, young wild boar, birds, and deer.

Clouded leopard

Tarsier

weird or what?

Each one of the tarsier's eyes is so big that each is heavier than the animal's brain. The size of its eyes provides excellent night vision.

No. A pangolin uses its long tongue to collect ants and termites.

Grasslands

In places that have more rain than deserts, but not enough for many trees, grasslands flourish. Grasslands are home to vast numbers of animals.

Lions on the prowl

Grasslands attract lots of grass-eating animals, which attract predators, including some of the most dangerous land animals in the world: lions.

Where in the world?

Grasslands cover huge areas of land. They are given different names, depending on where they are.

Northern Hemisphere
North American prairies
Asian steppes
Equator
African savanna
South American pampas
South African veld
Australian rangeland
Southern Hemisphere

Browsing on grass

Zebras roam the African savanna spending much of their days grazing in order to get enough of the nutrients they need.

A sprinkling of trees

If a grassland is dotted with trees, it's called a savanna. There are huge savannas in hot parts of the world.

How do grassland fires begin?

Grassland hazards

Severe weather changes and outbreaks of fire mean life in a grassland habitat can be tough.

Giraffes may look alike, but their patterned coat varies depending on where they are from.

Sun Some grasslands are hot, sunny, and very dry for much of the year.

Fire is a natural and important part of grassland life.

Wind sweeps across grasslands, since there are no trees to break its flow.

Tornadoes are a common occurrence on North American prairies.

Browsing on trees

Giraffes live on the African savanna, in areas where they can nibble on acacia and wild apricot trees.

Curiosity quiz

Look through the Grasslands pages and see if you can identify the picture clues below.

Become an expert... on a grassland's grazers and browsers, pages **50-51**

Some by lightning, and some by people who want to clear away dead growth.

A Sea of Grass

Most plants grow from the top, but grass grows from the bottom. This means it can grow back if it's eaten, or if it is flattened by being trampled.

Grass is resistant to being trample by hooves.

Grass clump

Grass shedding seed

Grass seed

Grass plants use the wind to spread their pollen (the fine dust that passes from male flowers to female flowers) and their seeds.

In summer, clouds of grass pollen give some people hay fever.

The cycle of life

Tropical grasslands have wet and dry seasons. In the dry season, the grass turns straw-colored and dies. With the rainy season, it springs back to life.

Cheetah

48

The grass we eat

Grass doesn't just provide food for animals, it provides food for us. In fact, most people's main food comes from grasses.

Sugar is produced from sugar cane, a giant tropical grass.

Corn is used for all sorts of food products, including tortillas.

Wheat is used for flour to make bread and cake, and for pasta.

Rice is a major food in Asia, and is eaten around the world.

Rye is mixed with wheat to make a heavy flour that is used for bread.

Texas bluebonnet

Spring flowers
While tropical grasslands burst into life in the rainy season, northern grasslands burst to life in the spring. The fields often contain colorful flowers.

Goosegrass seed

Grass attack

Walk through grass and you may find seeds clinging to your clothes. Some seeds cling with tiny hooks that work like Velcro.

Grassland trees often have flat bottoms, where animals have grazed.

Acacia tree

Giraffe

Baobab trees

In Africa, the baobab tree survives the blistering heat of the dry season by swelling and storing water in its trunk.

Some of them have been growing there for 3,000 years.

Grazers and Browsers

Grasslands are home to the largest herds, the biggest and fastest land animals, and the biggest birds on Earth.

Springbok grazing

Grazers

Huge herds of animals graze on grass. Grass is hard to digest, so grazers have bacteria in their guts that help with digestion.

White rhinocero

That one's white!

How do you tell the difference between a white and a black rhinoceros? White rhinos are grazers; they have wide, flat lips for nibbling grass.

Only the best

Wildebeest prefer young, tender grass. They have a special stomach where food stays for a while before being brought back to the mouth for a second chew.

Ostriches can grow to 9¼ ft (2.8 m).

Emus can grow to 6¼ ft (1.9 m).

Rheas can grow to 5 ft (1.5 m)

Wildebeest are a type of antelope.

Wildebeest

Big birds

Grasslands are home to the biggest birds in the world: ostriches in Africa, emus in Australia, and rheas in South America. All are flightless birds. The ostrich is the biggest of all.

What is the name given to animals that eat only plants?

Weaver bird

Woven home

Grass isn't just useful as a food, it can also be used as a building material. The weaver bird weaves strands of grass and torn leaves into a fabulous nest.

Weaver bird's nest

The nest has a trumpet-shaped entrance.

Become an expert...

on some of the predators who hunt the grazers, pages 52-53

Gerenuk

Browsers

Animals that eat bushes and trees are called browsers. The gerenuk is a browser, but one that can stand on its hind legs.

Black rhinoceros

This one's black!

Black rhinos are browsers; they have pointed lips for pulling leaves from bushes. Black rhinos are also known as hook-lipped rhinos.

A need for speed

There aren't many places to hide on grasslands, so animals rely on speed and stamina to escape.

Springboks look as if they are bouncing, as they spring away from predators.

Pronghorns are fast. They can run at 40 mph (65 km/h) and keep going for a while.

Zebras can also reach 40 mph (65 km/h), and will outrun most predators.

Wildebeest are large, but they can reach speeds of 50 mph (80 km/h) if needed.

Thomson's gazelle, like the springbok, will "bounce" in flight.

Ostriches can reach 45 mph (70 km/h), and keep going for about 30 minutes.

What a pushover

Elephants are also browsers. With their long trunks, they can reach higher than giraffes. If it's not too big, they will often push a tree over.

African elephant

They are herbivores.

Hunters and Scavengers

With so many plant-eating animals around, grasslands are a magnet to predators. Many hunt, but others prefer to scavenge: they pick over dead and rotting animals.

Team work

Lions are Africa's top grassland predators. By working together, they can hunt animals as big as buffalos and giraffes.

Stashing the prey

Predators will steal from each other if they can. To prevent this from happening, the leopard will drag its kill up into a tree. It can then eat undisturbed.

Leopard

On the brink

The rarest mammal in North America is the black-footed ferret, which hunts prairie dogs by chasing them through their burrows. Sadly, these ferrets are almost extinct.

Hunter

The cheetah is the fastest land animal in the world and can sprint at 60 mph (100 km/h) to chase prey.

Cheetah

Black-footed ferret

Are hyenas more closely related to cats or dogs?

Spotted hyena

Bone-breaker

Hyenas will eat up to one-third of their body weight at one meal. Their powerful jaws easily crush bone, and their stomachs can digest bone and hide, so little is left when they are finished eating.

Playing possum

Surely no predator could eat this rotten, stinking, dead opossum. Wrong—it's pretending to be dead, and it's made a foul smell to complete the impression.

The Virginia opossum may lie still for up to six hours until it feels safe again.

Virginia opossum

A bald head stays clean when meat is picked off a carcass.

Vulture

Scavenger

Vultures are scavengers, and they are not picky about the freshness of the meat they find.

Their closest relatives are the cats.

Going Underground

The animals shown below come from different continents and would never normally meet. However, they have one thing in common: they all use burrows.

Now you see it

Africa's aardvark is an amazingly quick digger. It can disappear into the ground in just five minutes.

Born to burrow

In Australia, a single wombat can dig a tunnel system with a total length of about 65 ft (20 m). It emerges at night to nibble on grasses and roots.

Common wombat

Rabbit's hole

Rabbits need to spend most of their time feeding, but they always stay close to their burrows.

Rabbit

A growing home

Rabbits can devastate large areas of farmland, not only by eating but also by digging extensive burrows.

Wombat's tunnel

Rabbit's nest

What animal's name means "earth pig" in Afrikaans?

Minibeasts

The animals that eat the most grass in grasslands are not the big herbivores but the tiny insects.

Ants often remove seeds. These tiny creatures are found all over the world.

Termites like these cut up plant matter and carry it back to their nests.

Crickets are predators, but they also eat grass, jumping from stem to stem.

Grasshoppers are vegetarians. Like crickets, they have large hind limbs.

Caterpillars need to eat and eat and eat. Many feed on particular plants.

Let's build a city
Black-tailed American prairie dogs dig long tunnels. Neighbors build next door, and the collection of tunnels soon becomes a "city."

Living with friends
In Africa, the banded mongoose leaves its hole to seek out termites—or perhaps a tasty bird's egg. It lives in communities of 15–20 individuals.

The banded mongoose can dig, but it often moves into old termite nests instead.

Banded mongoose

It's my hole now
Old prairie-dog holes may be taken over by small burrowing owls. They often stand outside and wait for a meal to walk past.

Burrowing owl

Burrowing snake
The American pine snake's pointed snout helps it to push its way through soft soil, but given the chance it will take over another animal's burrow.

Pocket gopher

Toothy grin
To keep dirt out of their mouths while they dig, pocket gophers can close their lips behind their front teeth. Their cheeks act like shopping bags, to store food.

Burrowing snake

Aardvark: "aarde" means "earth" and "vark" means "pig."

Termite Tower

Grasslands are home to billions of termites. Individuals gather together in huge colonies to build incredible nests.

How?

A king and queen start the towers. But nobody knows how the workers figure out what to do.

A look inside

A termite mound is full of tunnels and chambers. Like the rooms in a house, each has a particular purpose.

Warm air rises through the chimneys, pulling cool air in at the bottom.

Cooling chimneys

Some termites build chimneys into their towers. It's a built-in air-conditioning system.

Ground level

Edible fungi are grown in the fungus gardens.

Young termites are reared in nurseries that are at the heart of the nest.

Food stores

The inner chamber walls are made of soft, woody materials stuck together with termite droppings.

The king and queen live in the royal chamber. Workers bring food to them.

What's in the cellar?

Like many cellars, a termite's cellar is damp, but this dampness is caused by moisture as the termites respire. It's a source of cool air for the whole nest.

How many eggs will an African queen termite produce in her lifetime?

Who lives there?

A termite mound has four main residents: the soldiers, the workers, the queen, and the king.

Soldier termites

Soldiers

Some soldiers use jaws to bite attackers; others squirt a sticky glue. One kind of termite even has soldiers that block entrances by exploding.

These soldiers can squirt a sticky fluid through a nozzle-shaped head.

The king remains with the queen for life.

Keep on laying

A termite queen lives for up to 50 years, and, full-grown, is as big as your little finger. She depends on the workers. Her job is to lay eggs—up to 36,000 a day.

Workers

A mound's chief citizens are its workers. They build the mound a mouthful at a time, using mud, chewed plants, and their poop.

Worker termites

Giant termite mound

A large termite tower can take a minimum of ten years to build.

Shape variation

Termites build the biggest structures, relative to their size, of any land-living creature. There are different shapes.

Umbrella mound

Lunch time!

Anteaters love to eat termites. They collect as many as possible before the soldiers make their attack.

Weeds and wildflowers

Wildflowers are pretty, but some spread so rapidly they can be troublesome to farmers.

Ragwort is immensely poisonous to horses, ponies, donkeys, and cattle.

Thistle fruits have parachutes. The seeds may be carried far and wide.

English daisies hug the ground and do well in short grass (such as a lawn).

Cowslip is found in clearings and at the edge of woodland as well as in meadows.

Musk mallow produces pretty flowers from June to September.

Yellow bedstraw produces tiny, star-shaped flowers.

Field scabious can produce some 2,000 seeds per plant.

Clover is useful to farmers as it helps fertilize the soil. It is part of the pea family.

Dandelion heads are full of tiny petals, each of which turns into a seed.

Wood cranesbill is a woodland flower, but grows in hay meadows.

Buttercup flowers produce 30 seeds, so a large plant may have 22,000 seeds.

Life in a Meadow

In summer, a healthy grass meadow is like a jungle in miniature. It is packed with different plants and animals.

Hidden away
A meadow may be inhabited by moles—almost blind creatures that remain below the ground.

European mole

Under the surface

Moles are capable miners, tunneling long passages through the soil and producing telltale mounds of earth.

Campion flower

Watch out!
Crab spiders are powerful enough to catch bees and butterflies. They hide among the flowers, pouncing when prey comes close.

Crab spider

Get messy
 Make yourself a miniature meadow inside a jar. Sprinkle a few seeds onto damp soil. Put the jar on a windowsill, keep it watered, and watch as the seeds grow.

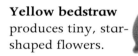

How long can a slow worm live? One, five, or 50 years?

Dandelion seeds

From flower to seed

Dandelions are frequently seen in meadows, since they have a way of spreading their seeds that is incredibly successful. Each seed has a parachute, to carry it far away.

The flower is ready to be pollinated by an insect.

The petals have died and the parachutes are forming.

A breeze lifts the parachutes. They may travel far.

Tiny monkeys

Harvest mice climb through the stems as ably as monkeys climb through trees. They build tennis-ball-sized nests.

Harvest mouse

A harvest mouse weighs no more than a teaspoonful of sugar.

Bubble blower

Froghopper nymphs create damp bubbles of sticky fluid to stop themselves from drying out. The bubble also protects the nymphs from being eaten.

There are many different types of snails, and a meadow is a good place to find a selection.

Slow but steady

The slow worm is not actually a worm; it's a type of lizard! But it has no legs. This one is hunting for a tasty worm or snail.

Slow worm

It can live for more than 50 years.

At the Water Hole

Meet my companion
Large animals often appear at a water hole with accompanying oxpeckers. These birds help the animal keep insects at bay, picking off ticks and leeches.

During the dry season in the savanna, the only reliable place to find water is at a water hole. It can be a busy place.

Impala

As well as insect control, oxpeckers clean up any wounds the host animal may have.

Red-billed oxpecker

That's better!
When a warthog takes a bath, it ends up dirtier than ever. The mud helps it to cool down and may help get rid of fleas and other nasty insects that infect the animal's skin.

Guinea fowl

Why are water holes such busy places?

Water birds

Birds are often seen wading in waterholes, looking for fish and frogs. There are many different types, and a few are shown here.

 Yellow-billed storks stir the water with a foot to disturb fish and frogs.

Saddle-billed storks are the largest storks, with a wingspan of 9 ft (2.7 m).

 Crowned cranes are the only cranes able to perch in trees.

Wattled cranes surround their large nests with moatlike water channels.

A never-ending thirst

Animals visit a water hole frequently, especially elephants. Elephants have to drink about 50 gallons (200 liters) a day.

Stuck in the mud

Some water holes dry up in the dry season. The African lungfish buries itself in a sticky bag of slime and hibernates until the rains come back.

A water hole is a cool place.

African elephant

Impala

Become an expert... on animals that have to conserve water, *pages 64-65*

In the dry season, a water hole may provide the only water for miles around.

Desert Regions

Deserts are Earth's driest places, with hardly any rainfall. That might sound like a nice climate, but it is very difficult to live in regions where water is scarce.

Sahara Desert
Gobi Desert
Sonoran Desert
Atacama Desert
Kalahari Desert
Great Sandy Desert

Weird weather

During the day, deserts can be scorchingly hot. At night, they can get incredibly cold. They often have huge sandstorms. Some deserts even have occasional snowstorms.

Deserts of the world

A quarter of our world is made up of deserts, the biggest one being the Sahara Desert in northern Africa.

Gray-banded king snake

Animal survivors

Few plants can survive in the desert, and so many animals are meat-eaters. Many deserts are also so hot that a large number of animals retreat underground during the day, hunting at night.

How tall is the tallest cactus on record?

Desert records

Deserts are full of extremes, so they hold quite a few impressive records.

 Rainfall: a desert must have less than 10 in (250 mm) of rain per year.

 Driest desert: is the Atacama Desert of South America.

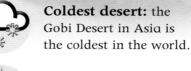 **Coldest desert:** the Gobi Desert in Asia is the coldest in the world.

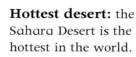 **Hottest desert:** the Sahara Desert is the hottest in the world.

Biggest desert: the Sahara Desert covers one-third of Africa.

Some cacti have spines instead of leaves, some have hairs. Spines protect the cactus from being eaten by animals.

Cactus

Curiosity quiz
Look through the Desert Regions pages and see if you can identify the picture clues below.

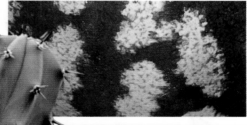

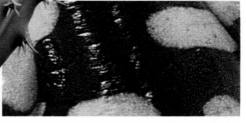

Plant survivors
It is very difficult for plants to survive without much rainfall. The cactus is a clever plant because it collects water when it rains and stores it for dry periods.

Become an expert...
on desert animals, pages **64-65**
on desert plants, pages **66-67**

to 65 ft (20 m) in the Sonoran Desert.

One Cardon cactus grew

Desert Animals

In order to survive, desert animals have developed ways of either keeping out of the heat, or cooling down.

Ouch

Keep your cool

Desert animals have a variety of ingenious methods for ensuring that they don't overheat.

A fennec fox loses heat through big ears. Furry soles help it to walk on hot sand.

Kangaroos lick their forearms to cool themselves down.

Gerbils stay underground in the heat of the day, emerging at night.

Tortoises will drool down their front legs to cool their body down.

Kalahari ground squirrels use their bushy tails as sunshades.

Turkey vultures urinate on their legs or fly up into cooler air if they overheat.

No water? No problem!

A camel can survive for about three weeks without water. When it does drink, it can take in a huge amount.

Apart from its hump, a camel has no fat under the skin, so it doesn't overheat.

Sand swimmer

The golden mole keeps out of the sun by "swimming" through sand, just below the surface. It rarely emerges, since it can find all it needs below the ground.

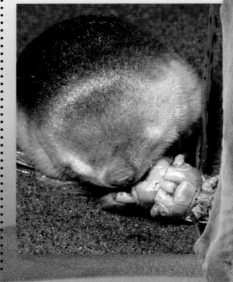

The trap is no larger than a marble.

Sand traps

This spider makes burrows in the sand and lines them with silk. At the top is a trapdoor. The burrow is an insect trap.

Trapdoor spider

Large, flat, well-cushioned feet help the camel to walk on sand.

What do you call a camel with one hump?

Sand-diving lizard

The lizard holds its feet away from the sand.

Hot sand?

If the sand becomes too hot, a sand-diving lizard will hold its feet in the air to cool down.

No problem!

The sidewinder adder slithers sideways, with only a small amount of its body pressed against the hot sand. It's a clever technique for keeping the snake cool.

A camel's hump contains fat that can be broken down to release water.

Long eyelashes

A camel's nostrils can close, to stop sand from getting into its lungs.

People have used camels for hundreds of years to cross desert regions.

The "ship of the desert."

Got you!

Antlion larvae trap insects by digging steep little holes. Insects fall in, tumbling straight into the fearsome jaws.

Antlion

I need a drink

When thirsty, the fog-basking beetle stands on its head. Fog condenses as dew on its body and trickles down to its mouth.

Channel that water

A thorny devil has a trick to help it cope. Grooves in its skin lead to the corners of its mouth. Dew collecting in the grooves runs straight to its mouth.

Thorny devil

A dromedary.

Desert Plants

Pebble plants

Life is tough for desert plants. It rarely rains, and whatever water a plant can find has to be stored and protected from thirsty animals.

Prickly plants

Cacti are unusual plants, many with spines instead of leaves. The main part of a cactus is its swollen, water-storing stem.

Cactus lookalike

Which of these two plants is a cactus? True cacti grow only in the Americas. In the deserts of Africa and Asia there are plants that look like cacti, but they belong to a different plant family.

Spines to protect the cactus.

Creases down side allow the cactus to swell and shrink.

Waxy surface prevents water from escaping.

Rounded shape reduces exposed area.

Swollen stem to store water.

Century plant

Is it a cactus?

Cactus

Spurge plant

Become an expert... on other types of plants, pages **58-59**

Is it really that old?
The century plant is so named because it supposedly lives for 100 years, then flowers once and dies. In fact, it lives for about 25 years.

Look! It's in flower!

How many species of cactus are there?

Old timers

Some desert plants grow slowly, but these tend to live a long time. In fact, deserts are home to some of the oldest plants in the world.

The **welwitschia plant** lives for up to 2,000 years.

Bristlecone pine trees live for up to 5,000 years.

Creosote bush [clones] live for up to 12,000 years.

Living stones

These "pebbles" are plants. They look like rocks so that thirsty animals won't eat them. Each pebble is actually a leaf. At the top of each leaf is a window that lets in light.

Tumbling along

Tumbleweeds spread their seeds by dropping them as they are blown by the wind. Because there are about a quarter of a million seeds per plant, some will grow.

Elephant's-foot plant

Water store

The elephant's-foot plant from Madagascar is so called because its stumpy stem looks like an elephant's foot that has been cut off. The stem is swollen with stored water.

Cotyledon

Blue echeveria

Watermelon

Life savers

Wild watermelons ripen underground and provide a source of water for desert-dwelling people who recognize the leaves.

Watermelons originated in southern Africa.

Moist and succulent

Plants with very fat leaves and stems for storing water are called succulents.

More than 1,600.

67

Rainfall and Oases

Desert animals and plants make the most of any rainfall, but they also thrive in oases, occasional islands of lush plant growth.

Why an oasis?

Oases form where an underground river comes close enough to the surface for plants to grow.

Couch's spadefoot toad

Tiny tadpoles.

Toad in the hole

Spadefoot toads can spend a year buried in the parched desert ground, hibernating. Their tadpoles have to grow quickly

A useful crop

In the Sahara, oases usually contain date palm trees. Many have been planted by people living there, for whom the date palm is the main source of food.

Dates

Not a welcome sight

Desert locusts normally live on their own, but after heavy rains they join to form vast swarms. A swarm may contain more than 50 billion locusts.

Giant barrel cactus

Are desert oases small?

Forever ready

Tadpole shrimp eggs can survive for more than 50 years. They hatch when it rains, and then grow, mate, and lay new eggs in just a few weeks.

Tadpole shrimp

Tadpole shrimp are called triops because they have three eyes.

I can survive!

Some salamanders have adapted well to living in deserts, which is surprising for an animal more usually found in damp conditions. They stay underground, venturing out after rain.

Tiger salamander

The largest land salamander

Cacti in bloom

Many cacti produce stunning flowers. Some of these will bloom for months, while some will last for just a few days.

Funnelform cactus flowers are shaped like a funnel, with a tube at the base.

Columnar cactus flowers, like many cacti, are pollinated by bees.

Queen of the night produces beautiful flowers as large as your hand.

Just waiting for rain

Many desert plants survive the bone-dry weather by avoiding it altogether. In dry conditions they exist as seeds. With rain, they rapidly sprout and flower.

Desert locust

Crocs in the rocks

Scientists have been amazed to discover crocodiles living in underground caves in areas of the Sahara Desert. They emerge when it rains to hunt.

Desert crocodile

Some oases are the size of a city.

After Dark

Once the sun sets, a desert changes.
Animals move into the open, all busily
hunting for something to eat.

Not the sun!

Scorpions are survivors. They
can survive freezing conditions,
not eat for a year, and even
stay underwater for three days.
But they can't stand bright sun.

Bat-eared
fox

Desert
scorpion

There's a fox around

Large ears help this African
fox to keep cool in desert
temperatures,
but also to hear the
insects on which it feeds.
It is on the prowl at night.

The wily coyote

Coyotes have adapted to
many habitats, including
deserts. They hunt by
feeling vibrations from small
underground animals and
uncovering them.

The coyote is
well known for
its distinctive
night-time howl.

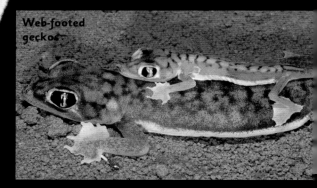

Web-footed
geckos

Coyote

Hungry tummies

Having spent the day in a tunnel,
these desert geckos are now hungry
for insects.

What's the word for animals that are active only around dusk or dawn?

Bat attack

This bat has hung out in a disused mine all day and has emerged to hunt for moths, caterpillars, crickets, and beetles.

White-lined sphinx moth

Night flight

The sphinx moth is as big as a hummingbird. It emerges at night to look for flowers such as orchids so it can feed on the nectar.

California leaf-nosed bat

Western coral snake

Scurrying spiders

Spiders are also active at night. This tarantula has killed a grasshopper.

Stay back!

The western coral snake is one of the deadliest snakes you could meet, with venom twice as powerful as a rattlesnake's. But because it's nocturnal, few people ever see one.

Tarantula

Crepuscular.

The Sonoran Desert

North America's Sonoran Desert is enormous. It also receives enough rainfall to support a huge variety of life.

Velvet ant

Is it a boy?
Velvet ants are actually wasps. Only the males have wings. Females lack wings, but they have a nasty sting.

weird or what?

The saguaro cactus, widely found in the Sonoran Desert, grows incredibly slowly— just 1 in (2.5 cm) a year. But it can reach heights of 50 ft (15 m)!

Gila woodpecker nesting in a saguaro cactus

Cactus homes
There are few trees in the Sonoran Desert, so the gila woodpecker makes its nest in a cactus stem. It will use the nest for just one year, before moving on.

Run, run, run
The most famous bird in the Sonoran Desert is the roadrunner, which scampers along at speeds of up to 18 mph (30 km/h), hunting small mammals, reptiles, and birds.

Roadrunner

Are there any forests in the Sonoran Desert?

A look at reptiles

From lizards to snakes to tortoises, many reptiles have successfully adapted to living in the Sonoran Desert.

 Gila monster This is one of the world's two venomous lizards.

 Desert tortoises spend 95 percent of their time underground.

 Rattlesnakes warn off predators by shaking a rattle on their tail.

 King snakes take their name from their ability to eat other snakes.

Ringtail cat

Is it a cat?

The ringtail cat isn't a cat: it's related to the raccoon. But it will clean itself very much like a cat.

Ringtail cats are nocturnal, emerging to hunt rats, mice, squirrels, frogs, and insects.

Saguaro cactus

Ready to expand

Following rain, this cactus's stem swells as the plant takes in water. It can absorb the weight in water of a small car.

Pig in the desert

A peccary may look like a pig, but it is only distantly related. Peccaries have poor eyesight, but a good sense of smell. They also produce a strong odor.

Collared peccary

There are no trees, but there are forests of saguaro cactuses.

Mountains and Caves

Mountains and caves are rocky habitats. The first offers exposure to all sorts of weather; the second offers shelter—but no sun.

Where in the world?

Earth has some impressive mountain ranges. The map shows the location of some of the best-known of these.

Mountain lion

Moving higher

Mountains support all sorts of animals. Many, like the mountain lion, have adapted to life on a mountain but are just as much at home in other, lower habitats.

By what other names is the mountain lion known?

Mountain weather

From rain to snow, when it comes to weather, a mountain is a place of extremes.

Temperature For every 330 ft (100 m) you climb, it gets 2°F (1°C) cooler.

Wind The strongest wind was 231 mph (372 km/h) on Mt. Washington, ME.

Rain Cherrapunji, India, receives about 40 ft (12 m) of rain a year.

Snow Mt. Rainier, WA, gets 58 ft (18 m) of snow a year.

Avalanche Snow collects on upper slopes, until the weight sends it tumbling.

Sun Often, one side of a mountain will be sunny while the other is rainy.

Formation of a cave

Caves form in areas with soft limestone rock. Over thousands of years, rainwater seeps through the soft rock, dissolving it. Gradually, small cracks become holes, and the holes become caverns.

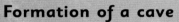

Curiosity quiz

Look through the Mountains & Caves pages and see if you can identify the picture clues below.

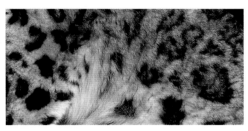

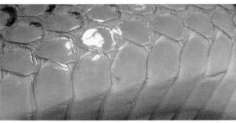

Become an expert...

on life in a cave, pages **78-79**

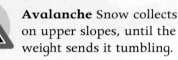

Puma, cougar, and panther.

Life in Thin Air

Walk up a mountain and you'll find that the habitat begins to change the higher you go. It also gets harder to breathe.

Become an expert...

on life in extreme cold, pages **10-11**
on deciduous forests, pages **18-19**

Mountain zones

A temperate mountain (a mountain in a cool part of the world) has distinct zones, each with its own wildlife.

A rare sight

There are thought to be fewer than 380 wild mountain gorillas. Although they look fearsome, gorillas are peaceful vegetarians.

Mountain gorilla

Alpine zone

In cool parts of the world, mountain peaks have a permanent coating of snow. Nothing grows at this height.

Alpine meadows

In the spring, as the snow begins to melt, lush meadows come alive with flowers. This zone is above the treeline.

Conifer trees

Conifers are adapted to surviving extreme cold. Even their shape protects against the weight of the snow.

Deciduous trees

Below the conifer trees, where the air gets a little warmer, grow the deciduous trees.

Alpine marmot

Time to wake up!

Mountain meadows are covered with snow in winter. Some animals, like marmots, survive this period by hibernating in burrows.

What is the meaning of the word "alpine"?

Rock gardens

When the snow melts in spring, the grassy meadows on high mountains are ablaze with flowers.

 Mountain daisy These bloom by the thousands across alpine meadows.

 Rock spiraea Creamy white flowers form dense mats over rocky areas.

 Thyme Low, thick clumps of miniature thyme have a colorful appearance.

 Saxifrage There are many different colors of this hardy plant.

 Edelweiss In many places, this plant is now protected: you can't pick it.

 Alpine snowbell Tiny bell-shaped flowers push their way up in early spring.

Gelada baboons

Alpine chough

Life in thin air

Mountain air is so thin that mountaineers need oxygen tanks. But birds like the chough have no problem breathing it. A chough once accompanied a climbing expedition to the summit of Mount Everest.

Who needs a tree?

Some monkeys prefer cliffs to trees! Gelada baboons actually sleep on cliffs, perched on the narrowest ledges.

Ibex

This is my home

Ibex are goats. They can scramble up the steepest slopes and leap around without losing their footing.

permanent snow.

Above the treeline and below

Cool Caves

A large cave will take thousands of years to form. From insects to bats, many animals find a cave a good place to live.

Stalactite

A dripping start

Caves are often damp, if not wet. Stalactites form drip by drip as minerals are deposited by water dripping from the roof.

A stalactite forms from the roof down.

Long-eared bat

I hear you!

Many bats have poor sight, but incredibly good hearing. They hunt by making squeaks and clicks that bounce off prey, telling the bat the prey's location.

Webbed skin for flight.

Cave spider

Feel the way

Like bats, cave spiders cannot see well. To compensate, they have a strongly developed sense of touch to help them move around—and catch prey.

What's the name for a person that lives only in caves?

All in white

Many cave dwellers, such as cave crayfish, are white because they need no protection from the sun's rays.

Drops of moisture show the bat is hibernating in a cold, damp cave.

Natterer's bat

Hunting for a snack

This southeast Asian snake will slip into caves because it knows there are tasty frogs, bats, and lizards to eat. Its slightly flat belly helps it to glide over rocks.

Sleep time

A cool cave is an ideal place for this bat to choose for its winter hibernation.

Red-tailed racer

A success story

Cockroaches are among the most successful of all living things, having inhabited Earth for more than 320 million years. Caves are just one of the habitats in which they thrive.

Cockroach

A troglodyte.

The Mighty Himalayas

The Himalayas are the world's highest range of mountains. They stretch 1,550 miles (2,500 km) across Asia.

On top of the world

The world's tallest mountain, Mount Everest, stands in the midst of the Himalayas.

Snow leopard

Look—it's a leopard

The snow leopard is probably the world's most rare and elusive cat. It lives high on mountains, including those of the Himalayas, far from human habitation.

Moon walk

Another Himalayan inhabitant is the black bear. This bear has a crescent-shaped white mark on its chest, resulting in its other name: moon bear.

Asiatic black bear

How high is Mount Everest?

It's a red panda!

The lesser panda is more closely related to the raccoon than it is to the giant panda. It lives in high bamboo forests, eating leaves, roots, fruits, and shoots.

Golden eagle

Poison flowers

Rhododendrons form eerie thickets in the Himalayas. Their gigantic flowers are beautiful, but toxic. Local bees collect the nectar to make a kind of honey that is poisonous to humans.

Talons ready!

The mighty golden eagle has a wingspan of more than 7 ft (2.3 m). A tasty pika would make a nice snack.

Wild rhododendrons

It's a rock bunny!

Pikas are small furry animals related to rabbits, though it's hard to spot a pika's tail! This one lives in mountain meadows and is well-adapted to cold weather.

Himalayan pika

It is 29,035 ft (8,850 m) high.

The Andes

Located in South America, the Andes are the world's longest chain of mountains, stretching some 4,500 miles (7,250 km).

Wet, wet, wet

While one side of the Andes is bone dry, the other is soaking wet jungle. This strange misty forest is called cloud forest.

Llama land

With their thick, shaggy coats, llamas can withstand extreme cold. They have been used in the Andes for centuries for their wool, meat, and milk.

Llama

Does the air get colder or warmer the higher up a mountain you go?

Flight of the condor

The world's largest bird of prey is the Andean condor. It has huge wings, but its size means it prefers to take off by leaping from a height and gliding on updrafts.

Andean condor

A bear wearing spectacles?

Despite its name, the spectacled bear does not wear glasses! It's named for the pale patches around its eyes. Unusually for a bear, it is largely vegetarian.

Hillstar hummingbird

Just so busy

Hummingbirds that live in the Andes mountains keep warm by staying active.

A hummingbird's heart may beat 1,300 times a minute.

Spectacled bear

It gets colder as you move higher.

Freshwater Habitats

Dragonfly

Freshwater habitats come in all forms. Some rivers, like the mighty South American Amazon, are incredibly wide. Other habitats are found in and around tiny streams.

Forty percent of all fish species live in fresh water.

It takes all kinds

From mammals and reptiles to mollusks and crustaceans, most groups of animals have freshwater representatives.

An animal's home

Fresh water is needed by all land-based life. Many animals, like the water shrew, make their home by water.

Is most of Earth's water fresh water?

Plants, too!

There is a huge range of aquatic freshwater plants, from duckweed to giant water lilies.

Duckweed are small, floating plants. They produce tiny flowers.

Water lilies are anchored to the bottom, but their large leaves float.

Reed warbler's nest

Some birds build their nests among rushes at the water's edge .

Tall cattails

Curiosity quiz

Look through the Freshwater pages and see if you can identify the picture clues below.

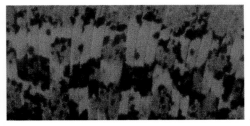

Become an expert... on life at a busy freshwater waterhole, pages **60-61**

85

The Flowing Current

From foamy white, cascading torrents to slow but ever-moving waters, rivers provide a rich habitat for a wide variety of wildlife.

The food chain begins

As leaves and dead animals fall into the waters, bacteria multiply. This brings food for aquatic larvae such as the caddisfly.

Caddisfly larva

Caddisfly

Mosses often grow on riverside rocks and trees and provide shelter for many tiny bugs that need damp conditions.

From small beginnings

Many rivers start life as fast-flowing streams. It is often a barren beginning, but plants and animals soon thrive.

Stop that water!

Beavers sometimes build dams to create lakes, slowing the flow of water and so changing their habitat. They also create lodges to live in.

Fallen trees can provide pathways for animals and insects to cross a fast-flowing stream.

Beaver

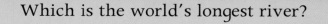

Which is the world's longest river?

The Colorado River

Changing the landscape

Over millions of years, rivers cut channels in the land. A notable example of this is the Colorado River and the Grand Canyon.

A brown bear is drawn to the river by the presence of salmon.

Brown bear

The fish is held in the bird's daggerlike beak.

Got it!

Many birds make a slow-moving river their hunting ground, snatching small fish from the water. The kingfisher is a colorful inhabitant of many European rivers.

Against the flow

Swift-flowing water captures oxygen, helping fish to breathe. Chinook salmon swim against the current heading for their spawning grounds. It's a dangerous journey.

The kingfisher will dive to about 10 in (25 cm) to grab a fish.

The Nile, in Africa, at 4,160 miles (6,695 km).

Still Waters

A freshwater lake is a large body of standing water. Lakes support a wide variety of life, especially at their edges.

Water hyacinth

Just floating around

Plants that float do well in still water, but they can take over. Water hyacinth looks pretty, but it is a fast-growing weed and can choke other life under a thick mat.

Floating plants such as water lettuce provide shade for a lake's creatures.

Water lettuce

Cat in the water

Catfish are named for their barbels, catlike whiskers that allow them to feel their way in murky water.

Bullhead catfish

Some species of catfish can grow to be more than 10 ft (3 m) in length.

Barbels help the fish to seek out prey. In the case of a large catfish, this may be a duck

Medicinal leech

Horse leech

Is it a sucker?

Wade in a muddy lake and you may emerge to find a leech on your foot. Some, but not all, leeches suck blood.

88

Which is the world's largest freshwater lake?

Is it a lake?

Lakes form in hollows, but not all are natural. A reservoir is a human-made lake, formed by a dam.

Ospreys are large birds of prey, reaching 5½ ft (1.7 m) wingtip to wingtip.

A cattail's flowers bloom on spikes and attract insects.

Attacks from above

Ospreys are found on all continents except Antarctica. They will nest near a lake or river, and swoop down to pluck fish from the water.

Pike

Life on the edge

Sedges and reeds often form a thick bed at a lake's edge. Known as emergents, they grow up from the lake floor and out into the air.

The ambush specialist

Pike are adept at ambushing their prey, lying in wait and nabbing passing frogs, fish, and insects.

Dragonflies are frequently seen on the plants at a lake's edge.

Don't mess with me!

The fearsome-looking alligator snapping turtle is the world's largest freshwater turtle. Some have weighed in at more than 220 lb (100 kg).

A slice of history

The common loon's ancestors lived on Earth some 65 million years ago. This red-eyed bird can dive to an incredible 90 ft (27 m) in search of food.

Lake Superior in North America.

Pond Life

A healthy pond is a magnet for life, both above and below the surface. It is full of fish, insects, and amphibians.

A frog emerges
From egg to frog is an interesting journey.

 Eggs are laid in jelly—up to 3,000 at a time. This is called frog spawn.

 Tadpoles hatch after 2-3 weeks. They breathe through external gills.

Back legs are the first to appear, followed by the arms.

 Froglets—young frogs—resemble their parents but are tiny.

Give a frog a couple of hours and it will darken its skin to match its surroundings.

Walking on water
Pond skaters are able to stride across the water's surface. Velvety hairs on their legs stop them from sinking. They hunt insects.

Pond skater

Not one to eat
A stickleback is named because sharp spines on its back make it an unpleasant mouthful for a larger fish.

Diving beetle larva

The male stickleback develops bright colors at nesting time. He protects the nest aggressively.

Larva here, larva there
The pond is busy with larvae, the young stage of an insect. A larva looks very different from its adult form.

Is the dragonfly good at flying?

I spy a dragon!

Dragonflies begin their lives in water, spending several years as nymphs, and molting as they grow. As nymphs and then as adults, they are fierce hunters.

Dragonfly

Too little space

These plate-shaped giant water lilies can measure up to 5 ft (1.5 m) across. Those pictured below are so successful that they are competing for light.

In hiding

Newts are shy and can be hard to spot. They creep around as if walking on tiptoe. Adult newts spend most of their life in damp places on land.

Water boatman

Mosquito larva

Mosquito larvae hang just below the water's surface, breathing air through a narrow tube.

Row, row, row your boat

With back legs that resemble oars, the water boatman looks as if it is rowing under water—though it hangs upside down to do so!

Diving beetles

Watch out!

The diving beetle is a fierce meat-eater. It dives down to snatch tadpoles and small fish.

A tank of air

The water spider is the only fully aquatic spider. It traps the air it needs in a silken bell. In other ways it behaves like any other spider.

Little builders

Caddisfly larvae build long, thin cases from sticks, small stones, bits of leaves, and grains of sand.

The caddisfly's case acts as a protective shell.

Caddisfly larva

Yes. A dragonfly can zip along at speeds of up to 17 mph (30 km/h).

Bogs and Marshes

Meat-eating plants

Carnivorous plants survive well in bogs and marshes, where the ground contains few nutrients.

The Venus flytrap catches its victims in a cage.

A bog or marsh is a wetland—a place where the ground is soaked or covered in water. It is a great place for wildlife.

This is a bog

Bogs form in cool, wet places, where the ground becomes spongy because it's full of rainwater.

Venus flytrap

Once an insect is caught, the leaf folds over it.

A natural sponge

Sphagnum moss keeps itself wet by soaking up rainwater. It has no true roots, so it absorbs water and nutrients.

Come on in, insects!

Cobra lilies thrive in boggy sites. These carnivorous plants trap insects in their tubelike leaves.

A sticky supper

Sundew plants catch insects with drops of sticky liquid that cover hairs on their leaves. It' an effective trap, but a sticky end for the bug.

In the past, what plant could have been used for dressing wounds?

This is a marsh

Marshes get their water from rivers that have spread over a wide area. Africa's Okavango Delta is a marsh.

Storks are excellent at fishing by stealth.

Yellow-billed stork

Wildlife paradise

A marsh is a haven for birds, reptiles, and mammals. There are more than 400 species of birds and over 150 species of reptile in the marshlands of the Okavango Delta.

Caimans are found in marshlands in Central and South America.

A caiman's jaws are strong enough to crush and shake food to tear off bite-sized pieces.

Caimans can hang with their body just below the surface, waiting for their prey to pass.

Caiman

When on land, a caiman's long limbs allow it to move faster than an alligator.

Waiting to kill

Caimans are efficient and powerful predators. They are closely related to crocodiles and alligators, but far smaller.

Become an expert...

on life in another wetland: a swamp, pages **94-95**

Where it grew, sphagnum moss was once used to dress wounds.

93

The Everglades

The wetlands of Florida are known as the Everglades. Parts of the area form a great big swamp that is very wet and always hot and steamy.

Summer rains

Summer is the rainy season in the Everglades. Plentiful rainfall makes the rivers swell, creating even more islands in this swampy wilderness.

Waders often have long necks that help them find food under water.

Birds

Waders are birds with long legs that allow them to walk in shallow water. There are many found in the watery Everglades, like this blue heron.

Manatees

Manatees are large mammals that live underwater. They are often called sea cows because they graze, like cows, on riverbed plants. They never come out of the water.

How long has the   American alligator lived on Earth?

Mangrove swamps

The mangrove is an unusual tree because it can live in shallow salt water. Many of these trees thrive along the coast where the Everglades meet the sea.

Is it grass or is it water?

Inland in the Everglades, the sawgrass plains can be found. In some areas, the water is barely visible because the sawgrass is so thick. The water is very shallow.

The menacing mosquito

The rainy summer of the Everglades triggers a mass hatching of 43 species of mosquitoes. These insects lay up to 10,000 eggs on an area the size of this page!

Mosquitoes possess needle-like mouthparts, used for piercing skin so they can suck blood.

Mosquito

Become an expert...

on other water mammals—whales and dolphins, pages **112-113**

This alligator is one of the most dangerous animals in the US.

The Everglades giant

The main hunters of this area are American alligators. They are huge, growing to 15 ft (4.5 m) long, and are the largest reptiles in North America.

The Everglades is the only place in the world where crocodiles and alligators exist together.

American alligator

About 25 million years.

Ocean Habitats

Earth's surface is more than two-thirds water. Large parts have little or no life. But elsewhere, oceans are bursting with activity.

Where in the world?

Our planet has five large oceans. They are large, and many parts of our oceans remain unexplored.

 Pacific Ocean Lying between the Americas and Asia, this is the largest ocean.

 Atlantic Ocean This lies between the Americas, and Europe and Africa.

 Arctic Ocean Frozen over for most of the year, this ocean is the smallest.

 Southern Ocean This area was only recognized as an ocean in 2000.

 Indian Ocean This is the third-largest ocean, covering 15% of Earth.

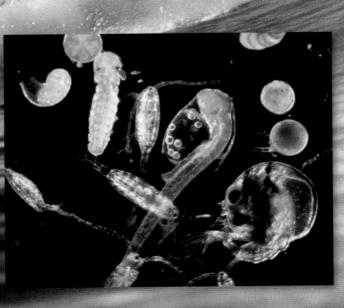

Food source

Plankton are algae and animals, many microscopic, that drift through the ocean, providing food for fish and other sea creatures.

What are the two main types of plankton?

Islands
Islands are important to oceans because life collects on and around them.

Some islands, such as Surtsey, are born following volcanic activity.

Ocean zones

Oceans are divided into zones according to depth. Some creatures stay in one zone, others move between zones.

Tidal zone

Open ocean

Tidal
This is the zone where the land meets the sea.

Spiny boxfish

Manta ray

600 ft (180 m)

Open ocean
Parts of the open ocean have very little life.

Twilight zone

Sperm whale

Squid

Sperm whales dive to the twilight zone in search of squid.

Twilight
A murky zone far below the sunlit surface waters.

3,300 ft (1,000 m)

Dark zone

Dark zone
No light hits this region, but sea creatures still survive.

Gulper eel

Hagfish

Abyssal zone
The ocean's deep, dark trenches.

Abyssal zone

Curiosity quiz
Look through the Ocean Habitats pages and see if you can identify the picture clues below.

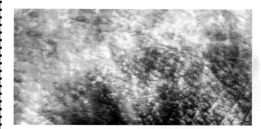

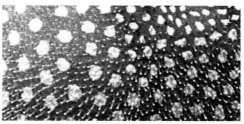

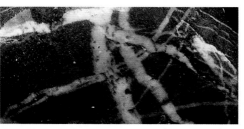

Become an expert...
on the twilight zone, pages 106-107

Phytoplankton (the algae) and zooplankton (the animals).

The Shoreline

The shoreline is the area where the land meets the sea. It's a tricky place to survive, with a constant battering by wind and waves, but many shorelines teem with life.

What type?

There are different types of shorelines. Some are shown below.

Sandy

These shores may look empty of life, but they are often full of small, burrowing creatures.

Plant life

Plants on a seashore have to be able to withstand strong winds and salty spray. They tend to grow low and grow behind the high tide mark.

Rocky

Rocky shores may have vertical cliffs, shallow platforms, or slopes littered with pebbles and boulders.

Muddy

Muddy shores are often found in estuaries, where a river flows into the ocean.

Plants such as thrift mark the top of the spray zone. The plant has long roots.

The tide rises and falls twice a day because of the Moon.

Where does white sand come from?

Limpet

Young oarweeds

Holdfasts are not roots. They don't take up food or water.

Hold tight!

Many shoreline seaweeds and animals have developed clever ways of staying put. They don't want to be washed away.

Like a limpet

It is almost impossible to dislodge a limpet. These shellfish use a muscular foot to cling to rocks and boulders.

The rock came too

Large, brown seaweeds use fingerlike holdfasts to grip a rocky surface. The hold is so firm that it is difficult to separate the seaweed from the rock.

Crabs can blend into the background very easily if threatened.

Over millions of years, shore pebbles are broken down by the constant battering of the sea.

Brown seaweed

Tidy up

Crabs provide a shore with its cleaners. Basically, they will eat whatever they can grab and hold, whether it is alive or dead.

Crab

Limpets hold water in their shells and create an airtight seal to survive exposure.

99

The sand on a tropical beach is formed from the crushed skeletons of coral polyps.

Rockpools

A rockpool is a miniature sea and home to many different creatures. Some stay in the pool permanently, but others get trapped there accidentally when the tide goes out.

The rocky shoreline

Rockpools form when the tide goes out and leaves sea water behind in rocky dips and crevices. For many creatures, this becomes their home.

Grab and flee

Gulls are scavengers and will take what they can grab. That includes fish, worms, and insects. They are often found inland as well as on the coast.

Black-headed gulls actually have white heads for much of the year.

A starfish "sees" by holding up the light-sensitive tips of its tentacles.

Black-headed gull in winter plumage

A gull's long legs help it to wade through shallow water in search of food.

A gull's feet are webbed so it can paddle when it's sitting on the water, like a duck.

A hard life

Life is tough in a rockpool. The temperature and saltiness of the water keep changing because of the weather. A small pool may dry out completely.

Can a sea anemone's   tentacles sting a person?

Local residents

Rockpools are home to many kinds of seaweeds and animals. Here are some of the most common.

Seaweed provides food for shellfish. Like plants, it uses sunlight to make food.

Mussels sieve food out of water. They close tightly if they sense danger.

Gobies are fish. This one can cover itself with sand in an instant.

Crabs search rockpools for the remains of dead animals, which they eat.

Shrimp can change color to blend in with their surroundings.

Shells may be empty, which means the creature that lived inside has died.

Starfish are hunters. They usually have five arms but no brain.

Anemones use their stinging tentacles to trap small animals to eat.

Mussels for dinner

Mussels are no problem for a starfish. It folds its arms around the shell and slowly pulls it open. Then it gobbles up the soft body inside.

Limpets cling very tightly to the rock if anything touches them.

Winkle

Seaweed provides a moist shelter where many animals can hide.

Limpet

Velvet crab

Strawberry anemones look like flowers, but they are animals.

The top of the velvet crab's shell is covered with velvety hairs.

If you touch a shrimp, it will dart away very quickly by flicking its tail and rowing with its legs.

Many kinds of sea anemone can sting you—it's best not to touch it if unsure.

The Coral Reef

Coral reefs are home to more than 15 percent of all fish species. Yet they cover less than one percent of Earth's surface.

Types of reefs

There are three main types of coral reefs: barrier, atoll, and fringing. Most grow in warm, shallow water, though there are cold-water reefs. The picture shows a barrier reef.

What is that?

A coral reef is made up from the stony skeletons of millions of tiny animals called polyps. Living polyps form a layer on top of these, and gradually, a reef forms.

Reef animals are brightly colored. Some are highly venomous

The older a reef, the wider the variety of animals living there.

Flat bodies help many of the smaller fish to slip between the corals for protection.

Angelfish

In the day, moray eels rarely emerge from the safety of holes in the coral.

Are corals animals or plants?

Is it hard...

With their stony base, hard corals are the reef-building corals. Most feed at night, their tentacles emerging to filter plankton from the water.

...or soft?

Soft corals grow long fronds that bend and sway in the underwater current. They tend to grow on overhangs and cliffs.

Odder and odder

From boxfish to frogfish, many of a coral reef's creatures have curious names that match their strange appearance.

Frogfish hunt by quickly opening their mouth to suck in a fish.

Sea slugs warn predators off by secreting an unpleasant mucus.

Spiny boxfish deter predators with their bony plates and tough spines.

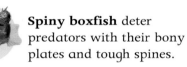
Sea cucumbers graze the sandy bottom of the reef, helping to keep it clean.

Cleaning time

Reef fish use "cleaning stations" to have their parasites removed by particular fish or shrimp. The cleaners are never eaten!

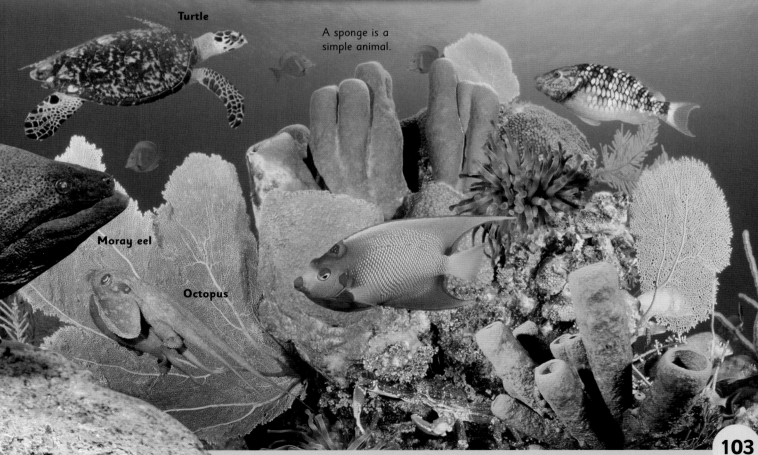

Turtle

A sponge is a simple animal.

Moray eel

Octopus

Corals are formed from tiny animals.

Ocean Habitats

A pufferfish sucks in water to swell its body.

Pufferfish

The BIG escape!

If threatened, a pufferfish may blow itself up with water so it cannot be swallowed by a predator, but most predators know to avoid these highly toxic fish.

Jellyfish protect themselves with stinging cells on their tentacles—but these don't stop a turtle!

Swim for my supper

Sea creatures such as the leatherback turtle will travel thousands of miles in search of jellyfish. If the food doesn't come to you, you have to go and find it!

The lion's-mane jellyfish is one of the largest of all jellyfish.

Become an expert...

on how animals survive difficult conditions on land, pages 26-27

It's a production line

Many sea creatures produce hundreds or even thousands of eggs to be sure some will survive. Turtles will lay 100 eggs at once, while a velvet crab may produce 180,000 eggs!

Velvet crab

Which of the creatures on this page has the longest history on Earth?

Survival in the Sea

The ocean can be a dangerous place, and sea creatures have developed a number of clever techniques to increase their chances of staying alive.

Blending in

Many of the ocean's inhabitants are masters of disguise.

Stonefish have lumpy, mottled skin that blends perfectly with the sea floor.

Pipefish swim upright, making them almost invisible among seagrass.

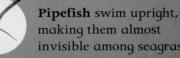

Leopard sharks have a pattern on their skin that helps them to hide.

On guard!

Some sea creatures will sting or attack if threatened. Lionfish spines contain venom that can paralyze or kill a fish. Divers are careful not to touch lionfish.

Lost in the crowd

Many smaller fish gather together in large schools. They then move as one unit to look larger than they would as a single fish. It can confuse a predator and so protect them.

Jellyfish are survivors. There were jellyfish in the oceans 650 million years ago.

The Twilight Zone

Diving deep below the sunlit surface waters, you enter the mysterious twilight zone and the light rapidly fades. Below about 600 ft (180 m), it gets as black as night.

Here's a big one

The twilight zone is colder than the sunlit zone, but some marine creatures have adapted to its harsh world. The largest visitor is the sperm whale, which heads down in search of squid.

Female anglerfish are the size

After taking a breath at the surface, the sperm whale will head down, reaching 3,300 ft (1,000 m) if necessary.

A fearsome-looking viperfish is hunting the mysid.

Many twilight-zone squid glow with bioluminescence—a light they produce.

Squid for supper

Twilight-zone squid provide food for many of the fish that live at this depth, but they are also efficient predators, able to grasp prey with their tentacles.

Eye-flash squid

Viperfish

How deep does the twilight zone go?

Going fishing

Deep-sea anglerfish patrol the very bottom of the twilight zone. The females are equipped with fishing rods.

Young anglerfish

Switch on the lights

Lanternfish have adapted to the dark by creating their own light. Different types of lanternfish have different light patterns, which helps them to find each other.

The anglerfish has its own fishing rod, equipped with luminous bait, to attract fish to investigate.

Lanternfish are the most common fish in the twilight zone.

of a grapefruit. Males are just 2 in (5 cm) long.

Red mysid will spit glowing fluid at a predator.

Giant red mysid

Color me red

Many twilight zone creatures are red. In the dark, red appears black, which helps the animal to hide from both prey and predators.

What big eyes

Large eyes help a twilight zone fish to see. Hatchetfish use large eyes to spot prey, but won't chase. As the prey passes, it's gobbled up.

Hatchetfish

Hatchetfish get their name from their axlike shape.

The twilight zone ends at about 3,300 ft (1,000 m).

The Deep

Animals living at the bottom of the ocean have to cope with dark, cold, and immense pressure. There's not much food, and the creatures grab what they can.

The gulper eel can stretch its stomach to take in prey larger than itself.

Open wide!

The gulper eel has adapted to its environment perfectly. With its large mouth, it doesn't miss an opportunity to seize prey that swims its way.

Gulper eel

The worms cannot feed like most animals, since they have no mouth and no intestine.

weird or what?

Hagfish are also known as slime eels, thanks to the huge amounts of gooey mucus they produce through pores on their bodies.

Ocean vents

Chimneylike vents build up in certain areas of the sea floor, creating mini communities. Bacteria thrive on the minerals at these spots and provide food for worms.

Do creatures at the base of deep-sea vents need sunlight to survive?

All mouth...
...with a long, long tail.

The gulper eel can survive at depths of more than 2 miles (3 km).

Hagfish

Full... for now

Hagfish have no true eyes and no jaws, but an unpleasant means of eating. When hungry, a hagfish will slide into a dead fish and start eating—from the inside out.

If it's dead, I'll eat it!

Rattail fish are scavengers, picking at the remains of animals on the sea floor. These fish grow slowly, taking 60 years to reach 2 ft (60 cm).

The gulper eel can unhinge its jaws to help take in a large fish.

A gulper eel's tail can stretch to almost 6 ft (2 meters) in length.

Giant tube worms!

Some of the tube worms that live at the base of deep-sea vents are as long as a person is tall. The worms have no mouths; they absorb minerals from the water.

These strange-looking creatures are the smallest lobsters in the world: squat lobsters.

Creatures living near vents do not need sunlight.

Icy Waters

The underside of the winter ice pack contains small algae-filled channels, which give it a curious green coloring. Many animals ???????? this harsh environment.

A perfect home

The Latin name for a harp seal means "the ice-lover from Greenland."

Seals are insulated from the icy waters by a thick layer of fatty blubber.

King penguin

A penguin cannot fly through the air, but it uses the same movement to "fly" through water.

Freezing? Not me!

The icefish is the only fish without red blood cells. This Atlantic crocodile icefish has a form of antifreeze in its blood to keep it from freezing.

Penguins have webbed feet.

Crocodile icefish

What are algae?

Krill

Krill are eaten by many marine animals, including baleen whales, icefish, and squid.

What's for supper?
Small, shrimplike krill feast on the algae when it is released from the ice in spring. They scrape the algae from under the ice.

Walrus

The mighty walrus
Walruses dive down to the bottom looking for large shellfish such as clams.

A walrus' tusks are used to anchor the walrus, to haul it out of the water, and for fighting.

I've got a bellyful!
After feeding on between 3,000 and 6,000 clams, a walrus will rest on the pack ice, warming up in the sun.

The powerful front limbs are used for pulling the walrus through the water.

Their feet act like rudders.

Another ice lover
Penguins are not found near harp seals or walruses, in the Arctic, but at the Antarctic. But like these animals, they are well adapted to life with ice.

Become an expert...
on the Arctic and Antarctic, pages **8-9** on penguins, pages **14-15**

Algae are plantlike organisms that require sunlight to make food.

Marine Mammals

Mammals are warm-blooded, have lungs (not gills), breathe air, and suckle their young. Human beings are mammals. So are whales, dolphins, and porpoises. As a group, these are the cetaceans.

Dolphins live in groups called schools. A school can contain 1,000 dolphins.

School of spotted dolphins

A sperm whale's teeth can grow up to 8 in (20 cm) in length.

Baleen plates are used to filter tiny shrimplike creatures from the water.

Sperm whale

Toothed whales

Some whales have teeth, and the largest toothed whale of all is the sperm whale. It spends its days diving deep in search of giant squid.

Humpback whale

Baleen whales

Baleen whales like the humpback have fringed brushes called baleen plates that grow in rows from their top jaw. They filter food with these.

Can cetaceans breathe underwater like fish?

What's for lunch?

Dolphins need to eat at least 22 lb (10 kg) of fish each day, swallowing them whole. When hungry, they will "herd" a shoal of fish together at the sea's surface before picking the fish off.

The thick pad, or melon, on the top of a dolphin's head helps to produce clicks.

Like all cetaceans, a dolphin's blowhole is on top of its head.

Porpoises

Porpoises are smaller than dolphins. There are six species.

Spectacled porpoises look as though they are wearing white spectacles.

Dall's porpoise is the largest porpoise, growing up to 7 ft 9 in (2.4 m).

Finless porpoises are the only ones that lack a dorsal (top) fin.

Harbor porpoises can often be spotted in shallow water, near harbors.

Vaquitas are the smallest of the porpoises, at just 4 ft (1.5 m) in length.

Burmeister's porpoise has a dark coloring, and a low dorsal fin.

Bottlenose dolphin

Echolocation

Dolphins talk to each other with clicks. The clicks also help a dolphin to find its prey. How? Because the noise bounces off objects in the water. It's called echolocation.

Blowing it

On surfacing, a whale breathes out rapidly, producing a spray of oily sea water called a "blow." They then take air into their lungs.

113

No. Cetaceans have lungs, not gills, and must come to the surface to breathe.

Look out! Danger!

Some marine creatures can kill or seriously injure divers, fishers, or swimmers. Here are some to avoid.

Sea snake venom is far more powerful than that of land snakes.

Cone shells are deadly poisonous to humans—never pick one up.

The **blue-ringed octopus** may be small, but its venom can rapidly kill a person.

A **box jellyfish's** sting is painful, and, unless treated immediately, lethal.

A box jellyfish has up to 15 tentacles on each corner.

Ocean Killers

Oceans are full of dangers, from small but effective biters and stingers to hungry sharks to the effects of humans.

Spiky invader

The crown-of-thorns starfish loves to eat coral. In fact, it loves it so much that if a community of these beasts moves onto a coral reef, they may strip it bare.

A great white shark has rows of razor-sharp teeth. If one is lost, another takes its place.

A fearsome reputation

Many people fear the great white shark, but attacks on humans are rare. However, sharks are fierce hunters.

Rich hunting grounds

These copper sharks have forced a school of fish into a tighter and tighter group. This makes it easier for the sharks to pick off the fish.

Copper shark

What is the largest shark (and the largest fish) in the world?

Oil spills

A coastal oil spill is a disaster for wildlife. The oil floats on the sea's surface until it is carried to land. It will coat everything it touches.

Killers can come from above. Many seabirds can swoop into the water and grab a fish or crab.

Oil clogs up a bird's feathers, leaving it unable to stay warm.

Razorbill

Taking too much

The biggest threat to ocean habitats comes from people, through overfishing and pollution. If too many fish are taken, there is no chance for stocks to recover.

Some fish populations have been fished to the point of extinction and won't recover.

The big one

Giant waves called tsunamis occasionally cause devastation to coastal communities. Buildings and boats are tossed around and crushed.

The whale shark.

Mangrove Swamps

Tropical swamps are good places for mangrove trees. These trees have roots that stick out of the water like stilts.

The roots take in oxygen from the air.

Too much salt?

Mangrove trees get rid of excess salt by concentrating it in dying leaves, and in the bark. Some is filtered out through the roots.

Nature's nursery

As well as providing support, the dense network of twisting mangrove roots provides a safe nursery for young fish, shellfish, and crustaceans.

The archerfish can squirt bugs above the water, making them drop into the swamp.

A mudskipper's front fins are used like legs.

A walking fish

The mudskipper is actually a fish, but it can survive long periods out of water. It does this by storing water in large gill chambers.

Can mangrove trees grow in fresh water?

One to avoid...

In Australia and Asia, the saltwater crocodile often makes its home in mangrove swamps. Males can reach 20–23 ft (6–7 meters) in length.

Ready to go it alone

Some mangrove seedlings grow while attached to the parent plant. When ready, they fall and float away, until they find a suitable place to lodge in mud.

Dead mangrove leaves contain salt the tree needs to lose.

A crab for supper

Long-tailed macaques, also known as crab-eating monkeys, are one of the larger inhabitants of Indonesian mangrove swamps.

A slick escape
Long-tailed macaques are so well adapted to life in a mangrove swamp that they will happily jump into the water to escape a predator's clutches.

Yes, but they have no competition from other trees in salt water.

Towns and Cities

Nature always manages to find its way into our towns and cities. In fact, left alone, it can quickly take over.

Where in the world?

Nighttime satellite images show many of the world's cities, though only those where electricity is widely used.

Seagull

Animals
Wild animals such as the red fox have quickly learned to live alongside human beings. They know we throw away tasty things.

Red fox

Birds
Many people leave food out for birds. Some, like seagulls, have become pests, brave enough to snatch food from a hand and leaving droppings in return.

What is the current world population of human beings?

Plants

Sycamore tree seedling

Concrete and heavy paving slabs are no barrier to plants, however tiny. A small plant does no damage, but as it gets larger, its roots will push up paved areas.

Gulls are commonly seen, both on coasts and inland.

City life

If you live in a city, it may look barren of wildlife, but birds, insects, and larger animals will be all around.

Curiosity quiz

Look through the Towns and Cities pages and see if you can identify the picture clues below.

Become an expert...

on the insects that invade our homes, pages **122-123**

Outdoors

Many animals have adapted to living in close proximity to human beings. They are frequently spotted in cities—but they remain wild.

Black rat

A plague of rats

Black rats spread around the world on ships, and now live everywhere that people live. They love to live in sewers.

I spy a fox!

Foxes like the edges of cities, where yards are bigger and wasteland is a bit wilder. But they also survive in more built-up areas.

Red fox with cubs

Red foxes are equally at home on the Arctic tundra as they are in a city.

Masked bandits

Raccoons have nimble little hands that are perfect for opening plastic or paper packages and unscrewing the lids on jars.

Black fur makes the raccoon appear masked.

Common raccoon

What historical event is the black rat famous for?

Yummy—garbage!

Gulls adore garbage dumps. Rotting food and soiled diapers attract maggots, forming a tasty mix to a seagull.

Rats will eat almost anything.

Urban invaders

Weeds are unwanted wild plants that compete with garden plants (and crops) for space.

Burdock spreads its seeds by means of tiny burs, which catch on animal fur.

Fireweed takes its name from its rapid growth in some areas after a fire.

Stinging nettles have many uses, but they can take over a patch of land.

City pigeon

The pesky pigeon

City pigeons are the descendants of rock doves, which used to nest on seaside cliffs. Ledges on roofs are much the same.

A miniature garden

People plant window boxes to add color to their houses, but these small habitats also attract bees, butterflies, and other insects.

Moose on the loose

Anchorage, Alaska, has a population of more than 1,000 urban moose. They graze in people's backyards and are a hazard on the roads.

Bees and butterflies spread a plant's pollen.

Anchorage moose are a danger on the roads.

ATTENTION!

Bubonic plague. Their fleas spread plague to Europe in the 1300s.

Indoors

You probably see insects, or larger animals, in your home every day. There are more than you think!

In the dust

Dust mites are found in homes everywhere. These microscopic animals feed on the dead skin that you shed every day, finding it amid the dust and fluff at your feet.

In the cellar

Black widow spiders like the dark spaces under floorboards. Their bite contains a nerve poison that can paralyze your muscles and cause agonizing pain.

The black widow is the most deadly spider in North America.

Black widow

In the flour

Tiny beetles find their way into open packets of flour, pasta, rice, or cookies and lay microscopic eggs that hatch into grubs.

Flour beetle grubs

Flour beetle

House mouse

There's a mouse in the house

House mice hide in walls or under old floorboards and only come out when the room is quiet. They wriggle up the tight gaps between cupboards and walls to get onto countertops.

How long can a cockroach live without its head?

In the attic

If you've ever been stung by a wasp, you'll know how painful it is. Some wasps will build their papery nests in attics or behind house shutters. They may contain 5,000 wasps.

Wasp

Wasps' nest

Deathwatch beetle

What else?

Many other creatures inhabit homes around the world. Here are a few more.

Deathwatch beetle larva

Deathwatch beetle larvae can destroy a timber beam with their tiny holes.

Clothes moth caterpillars chew into woolen jumpers and fur coats.

Bed bugs are bloodsucking insects that can infest beds, feasting at night.

Silverfish digest paper, so cardboard packaging and boxes are food to them.

Cockroaches love warm, damp places, and will eat just about anything.

Carpet beetle grubs eat the wool fibers in carpets, turning the wool to sugar.

Craneflies often enter homes. They look like huge mosquitoes but don't bite.

Gecko In Asia, geckos are sometimes welcomed—they eat insects and spiders.

Booklice can be found chewing on stored flour, or on paper—hence their name.

In the wood

Woodworms are not worms but beetle larvae. They eat dead trees in the wild, but wooden floorboards and beams are as good. One type is the deathwatch beetle larvae.

Housefly

Houseflies eat by "spitting" on food to make it mushy, and then sucking it up through a spongy proboscis.

Housefly

Houseflies can taste with their feet.

About seven days.

123

Index

Index

Picture credits

The publisher would like to thank the following for their kind permission to reproduce their photographs:

(Key: a-above; b-below/bottom; c-center; f-far; l-left; r-right; t-top)

Alamy Images: Oote Boe 118-119; Rachael Bowes 57bl; Nigel Cattlin 123l (Booklice); Danita Delimont 72l, 72br; James Osmond 119t; Pictorial Press 69crb; Kevin Schafer 43br; James D. Watt 97cr; Gunter Ziesler 57br; **Bryan and Cherry Alexander Photography:** 11cr, 12bc, 13tr, 13br; **Ardea.com:** Brian Bevan 16l, 17cr; Jean-Paul Ferrero 44cr; Bob Gibbons 100tl; Jean Michel Labat 46bc; Stefan Meyers 86clb; Ron & Valerie Taylor 104cl; Zdenek Tunka 87bc, cl; M. Watson 23tr; **Bat Conservation International:** Merlin D. Tuttle 71; **Steve Bloom/ stevebloom.com:** 93cl, tl; Corbis: Theo Allofs 98cb; Craig Aurness 119crb, 121bl; B.S.P.I 102tr; Anthony Bannister 123l (Bed bug); Tom Brakefield 51fcrb; Suzanne Brookens 56t, 57c; Ralph A. Clevenger 9t; Brandon D. Cole 97bc (Hagfish), 109cl; W. Perry Conway 55tl; Peter McDiarmud/Reuters 39fcrb (stick insect); Douglas Faulkner 94bc; Michael & Patricia Fogden 24br, 33bc; D. Robert & Lorri Franz 52bl; Farrell Grahan 94c; (Springbok), Martin Harvey 51fcr, 54bl; Hal Horwitz 67cra (Bristlecone); George H. H. Huey 67cra (Creosote); Gallo Images 33c; 56tl; Gavriel Jecan 47br, 51; Peter Johnson 12cr, 51br, 57tr, 60bl, 61cla; Frans Lanting 42tr; George D. Lepp 65cr; Joe Macdonald 51fcr (Pronghorn), 53tr; George McCarthy 24tr; David Muench 62cla, 95l; Carl & Ann Purcell 95tr; Jeffrey L. Rotman 50cr; Gallen Rowen 9tr, 15tl; Kevin Schafer 34cr, 51cl; Paul A. Souders 6bl, 48-49; Kennan Ward 11tr; Chad Weckler 49tr; Ralph White 108-109b, 109tr; Tony Wilson-Bligh / Papilio 7fcrb; Winfred Wisniewski/ FLPA 14cl; Michael de Young 10tl, 66, 81br, 87cra,103cra; **DK Images:** Natural History Museum 30ca, 45tl; **FLPA - images of nature:** Thomas Mangelsen/Minden Pictures 26cb; Gerry Ellis/Minden Pictures 22c, 73bl; Danny Ellinger/Photo Natura 73br; Michael & Patricia Fogden/ Minden Pictures 37c (Rain Frog), 40tl, 40bl; 41l; Slivestris Fotoservice 30bl; Mitsuhiko Imamori 38br; Heidi & Hans Juergen-Kochs 42-43b; Frans Lanting/ Minden Pictures 28-29, 35br, 44bl; 82tl; Flip Nicklin/Minden Pictures 42l; Mark Moffett/Minden Pictures 21bc; Tui De Roy/Minden Pictures 29br, 74-75, 80-81; Jurgen & Christine Sohns 80br, 81tl; Albert Visage 31cra, 34bl; Terry Whittaker 44ca; Konrad Wothe/Minden Pictures 77cr; Norbert Wu/Minden Pictures 97bc, 106br, 107bc, 108-109; **Getty Images:** 121cr; Aquavision 102br; Daryl Balfour 48cr; Gary Bell 18; Peter Bisset 94tl; Tom Brakefield 45bl; Ian Cartwright 75bl; John Chard 62-63; Stuart Cohen 75crb; Daniel J. Cox 35tr; Paolo Curto 112cb; Siegfried Eigstler 58-59b; Timothy Hearsum 72-73; Gerald Hind 53; Steven Hunt 97fcr, 104tl; Jeff Hunter 102; Russell Illig 75c; Panoramic Images 61tl; Lonny Kalfus 1l ; Michael Kelley 87tl; Frank Lemmens 6tl, 68-69; David de Lossy 76cb; Alan Majchrowicz 27tr; Margaret Mead 37tr; Jeff Mermelstein 121t; Marvin E. Newman 94bl; Michael K. Nichols 75br, 76bl; Paul Nicklen 8b, 97fcra, 111r, 128b; Joseph Van Os 15bl, 27bl, 28c, 52cl; Ben Osbourne 15br; Yoshio Otsuka 49; Michael S. Quinton 89crb; Norbert Rosing 16, 111cl; Jeff Rotman 105; Rubberball 76bc; Brian J. Skerry 110; Stockbyte 96; Stephen Studd 17crb, 18cr; Keren Su 27br; Harald Sund 4cla, 22l; Medford Taylor 116tl; 117tr; Roy Toft 23cl, 23br; Stuart Westmoreland 103tl; Art Wolfe 9cr, 14br, 15tc, 15tr, 52tr; Jeremy Woodhouse 70bl; Paul A. Zahl 107br; **Image Quest Marine:** 107tc, tr ; **Magnum:** Paolo Pellegrin 115bl; **N.H.P.A.:** 60-61b, 67tc; Anthony Bannister 54tr; Bill Coster 27tl; Stephen Dalton 36c, 84clb; Jeff Goodman 50br; Martin Harvey 50l,115r; Brian Hawkes 97tl; Adrian Hepworth 30-31; Daniel Heuclin 37c (Surinam Toad), 37tl, 61tr; T. Kitchin & V. Hurst 74b; Hellio Van Ingen 11br; Michael Leach 118bl; A.N.T. Photo Library 28tr, 37c (Gastric brooding frog); Lutra 88bl; Kevin Schafer 73; **Natural Visions:** Heather Angel 21c, 21clb; Richard Coomber 60c; **Nature Picture Library:** 71r; Pete Cairns 89ca; Adrian Davies 91br; Jurgen Freund 116c, 117tl; Barry Mansell 79cla; Anup Shah 117bl, 117br; David Shale 107c; **Photolibrary.com:** Doug Allan 110b; Kathie Atkinson 63tr, 65br; IFA Bilderteam 77tc; Michael Fogden 64tr, 64cb, 65bc; Nick Gordon 40cl; Rodger Jackman 63bl, 68cra, 68c; Mark Jones 83cla; Brian Kenney 70br; Scripps Inst. Oceanography 109br; OSF 96bc; **Planetary Visions:** 4-5c; **Science Photo Library:** 25fcl; British Antarctic Survey 9br, 15cr; B. Murton / Southampton Oceanography Centre 108l; Kenneth Librecht 14tl; Tom McHugh 55bl; David Scharf 119fcrb, 123l (Carpet beetle); Eye of Science 49cr; Sheila Terry 102c; **Seapics.com:** 97cr (whale), 97fbr, 97fbr (squid), 103c, 106tr, 106cl, 106c, 106bl, 112t, 112cl, 112bc, 113l, 113br, 114bl, 114br, 115tl; **Still Pictures:** C. Allan Morgan 39fcrb (click beetle); Michael Sewell 39clb; **Zefa Visual Media:** Winfried Wisniewski 51fcrb (Gazelle)

All other images © Dorling Kindersley For further information, see www. dkimages.com

Acknowledgments

Dorling Kindersley would like to thank: Lorrie Mack and Fleur Star for proofreading, Ian Sherratt for production assistance, Helen Stallion for additional picture research, Martin Copeland and Rob Nunn for picture library assistance, and Gemma Fletcher for design assistance.